Corporate Reputation

Corporate Reputation

12 Steps to Safeguarding and Recovering Reputation

Leslie Gaines-Ross

John Wiley & Sons, Inc.

Library of Congress Cataloging-in-Publication Data:

Gaines-Ross, Leslie.
   Corporate reputation: 12 steps to safeguarding and recovering reputation/Leslie Gaines-Ross.
     p. cm.
   Includes bibliographical references and index.
   ISBN 978-0-470-17150-9 (cloth)
1. Corporate image. 2. Responsibility. 3. Corporations—Public relations. 4. Organizational effectiveness. I. Title. II. Title: 12 steps to safeguarding and recovering reputation. III. Title: Twelve steps to safeguarding and recovering reputation.
   HD59.2.G35 2008
   659.2—dc22

                          2007038101

To my father, who safeguarded me forever

CONTENTS

ACKNOWLEDGMENTS

Leading greeting card retailer Hallmark reports that more people are writing thank you notes. Yet, of the six billion cards that Americans buy each year, only 3 percent contain words of thanks. If people only had the time, that 3 percent would be closer to 30 percent.

One of the best things about writing a book is that saying thanks is not a matter of making time. It is an integral part of nearly 100 percent of all books published. An author wants to do her "thank yous," for a book without an acknowledgment is like a birthday cake without a candle.

Acknowledgments are therefore an important matter, and I write it now with due care and the utmost gratitude.

Thank you to my colleagues at Weber Shandwick who welcomed and embraced me from day one. Special appreciation goes to Weber Shandwick President Andy Polansky for the constant support he has shown me in countless ways. Gratitude also goes to Weber Shandwick CEO Harris Diamond and Chairman Jack Leslie for creating an organization that values intellectual capital and celebrates collaboration. Other Weber Shandwick colleagues who have provided their time, insights, and encouragement are team members Elizabeth Rizzo and Meghan Paul.

Extraordinary thanks go to Mark Murray, whose friendship, loyalty, and editorial expertise never cease to amaze me. Barely a day goes by without his superb writing skills transforming mangled sentences into magnificent prose. More important, he is a man of immeasurable thoughtfulness. His kind heart and trustworthiness make him a friend for life.

My steadfast circle of friends deserves special mention as writing this book comes to a close. Thanks to Marilyn Platzer, who always makes things better and who compassionately declined to scold me for even thinking about writing yet another book. Many thanks also go to my friend and former colleague Carol Ballock, who shares my intense interest in reputation and whose insights are always dazzling and deeply appreciated. Several other friends who supported my efforts include Ron Alsop, Lina Di Blasio, Joy Sever, Charles Fombrun, Chris Komisarjevsky, and Per Heggenes. Thanks also go to Weber Shandwick colleagues Jill Surdyka and Loretta Nauth.

I extend appreciation to my editor Tim Burgard at John Wiley & Sons for believing that I would actually meet this deadline and having confidence that the topic of reputation continues to hold value for readers.

Thank you to the many business professionals who shed light on their experiences with safeguarding and recovering reputation—Entergy Director of Utility Communications Sandra Alstadt, Indiana University School of Journalism professor and former public relations officer Jim Bright, Nielsen BuzzMetrics CEO Jonathan Carson, Tyco International VP of Advertising and Branding Jim Harman, consultant and former public relations officer Jon Harmon, and from Dow Jones's Factiva, Chris Shaw and David Breg. Credit goes to the many CEOs, colleagues, and corporate communications officers who cannot be mentioned here but whom I have learned from every day in the course of my career.

Untold thanks are reserved for my parents, who provided me with a model of industriousness, boundless energy, and love of business. Although my father passed away before this book was finished, I know he would have been immensely proud of me. It would have been a great joy to hand him a second book to show his friends as they walked in the door at Half Moon Lane.

As I look back on the many months of weekends lost because of time spent writing, I know that I should have sent hundreds of thank you notes to my husband Dan and our children for their patience. But, alas, I never made the time. I do now. They deserve my profound gratitude and apologies for listening to endless moans about "the book" and for cherishing those few times that I managed to spare when we could all be together. To Dan, thank you again and again and then some. To Allison, Ben, Miles, Hannah, Emma, and Hudson—I promised you multitudes of weekends after finishing my first book and failed miserably at keeping my promise. Now I mean it.

PREFACE

Everything in reputation management is very simple, but nothing in
reputation management is very easy.

WHY I WROTE THIS BOOK

For over two decades, I have been a "reputation" watchdog, seeking out
the most subtle references to corporate reputation in magazines, newspapers, journals, online media, and books. I have also been a keen and
vigilant observer. Now, after so many years, my hard-copy manila folders
are bursting with clipped articles and my ever-expanding computerized
corporatereputation.doc file threatens to engulf my hard drive's very
last gigabyte.

Years ago, when I first began my inventory of articles, speeches,
newspaper headlines, and books, my manila folders were few in number
and tagged with labels limited in breadth—"Corporate Advertising,"
"Tylenol Crisis," "Brand Coca-Cola," "Most Admired Merck," "Power
Brands," and "Companies to Watch." Although at this time a few
corporate crises had begun to raise eyebrows, interest in such incidents
was for the most part confined to narrowly defined audiences who read
the business sections of national newspapers and business magazines.

Crises that today directly impact a company's reputation and fortunes rarely made it into the public consciousness.

As the millennium approached, however, interest in reputation mushroomed and my folders, both hard copy and digital, multiplied exponentially. My new folders now had upbeat titles such as "Digital Companies," "Built-to-Last Companies," "Wall Street Darlings," "Euro-Companies," "Fast Companies," "IPO Companies," and "Best Companies to Work For." I now even had folders labeled "New CEOs," "Under 25 CEOs," "CEO Challenges," "CEO Stats," and "CEO Brands." In the midst of my quest to always keep my folder-naming up to date, I had a sudden epiphany. I realized that my mushrooming filing responsibilities directly reflected the new importance being given to corporate reputation by the wider business and nonbusiness communities.

The briefest of inquiries soon confirmed my file-inspired hunch. From the beginning of the 1990s, major U.S. media's usage of the term *reputation* had tripled. In 1996, New York University professor Charles Fombrun authored his seminal work, *Reputation: Realizing Value from the Corporate Image*.[1] Interest in *Fortune*'s Most Admired Companies and Best Places to Work survey rankings also grew red hot. Confirming that a broad market existed for the study of corporate reputation, *Fortune* began selling these rankings to more and more companies seeking to build better reputations.

Based on all this accumulated data and critical focus on reputation, I have made an important discovery—the "science" of reputation management has entered a new era. What had begun as a barely noticeable ripple in the sea of business has grown into a rising tidal wave that now sweeps across businesses in every region on earth. Reputation management is now accepted as a distinct body of knowledge, and the study of protecting and recovering reputation is drawing universal interest, not only among business audiences, but also the general public.

Surely, part of the reason for this radical shift in reputation's appeal was the rise of fashionable dot-com companies in the late 1990s. Led by baby-faced entrepreneurs who built company reputations overnight with too-often empty promises rather than sustainable bottom lines, business suddenly became highly entertaining and great cocktail party conversation. With a bull market and 401(k)s to invest, the public and investors paid rapt attention to the latest corporate maneuvers and company success and failure. They also began to take a genuine interest in specific companies and industries, watching their every move, often for both financial and personal reasons. It was the soap opera *As the World Turns* and the television program *The Millionaire* all rolled into one. However, more was yet to come, which would raise the level of interest in business reputation from a spectacle to something more serious and useful.

As the twenty-first century took root, the study of reputation became far more rigorous, suggesting for the first time that building corporate reputation was becoming something more than a passing trend. Business professionals began viewing reputation management as a learned skill with characteristics that could be isolated and studied as a body of knowledge, much like other business practices and operations. To complete the cycle, however, the upside of reputation management, as represented by the rise of the dot-coms, was soon to be tempered by the downside of reputation failure. It became startlingly clear that knowing how to build a reputation was not enough. Knowing how to protect and salvage a lost reputation was also critical.

The defining moment came in 2002, a year of multiple corporate scandals, including the infamous Enron debacle and the mass demise of Internet start-ups. So overwhelming were these tumultuous, reputation-shattering events that I was driven to adopt an entirely new file-labeling nomenclature: "Dot Bombs," "Pre-Enron," "Post-Enron," "Anti-CEOs," "CEO Turnover," "Boomerang CEOs," "NGOs," "Web Activists," "Corporate Apologies," "Crisis Management," "Reputation Risk," "Board Reputation," "Government Intervention," "SarbOx," "Shareholder Activists," and "Reputation Failure." During this post-dot-com and post-Enron period, the ruins of once-heralded industry leaders, corporate failures, and lost investments defaced a formerly pristine business landscape. Suddenly, all corporations and CEOs were vulnerable. Corporate propriety became a matter of overriding concern. Corporate and societal interest in reputation management became intense.

With corporate disasters seemingly everywhere, and with the business community now tainted in the eyes of the general public and generally devoid of credibility, the study of reputation became a legitimate body of knowledge with emerging new disciplines. One of these distinctive disciplines that I termed was "Reputation Recovery"—the study of the ill effects of organizational failure and the steps needed to counter, stabilize, rebuild, and safeguard company reputation. Even though company crises have always been with us—the Three Mile Island nuclear reactor incident and the Tylenol poisonings, for example—the sheer number and magnitude of corporate stumbles and falls from grace since 2002 magnified the need for a viable framework for the repair and recovery of damaged company reputations. It was then that a new genre in the reputation field was born.

As whistle-blowers, e-mail trails, deliberate leaks, and bloggers emerged, it became apparent that corporate downfalls were neither born overnight nor accidental. A lengthy trail of missed or misinterpreted signals usually preceded a crisis. By isolating and identifying these overlooked warnings, experts believed they could establish ways to diminish, if not prevent, reputation-damaging crises before they occurred, and if they did occur, make sure they were never repeated.

Moreover, while common business wisdom had always assumed that an organization would rebound from an incident within two years due to the inevitable waning of public interest, research now showed that such an assumption was no longer true. In an age of 24/7 media coverage, the Internet, and always-on communications, coupled with the public's growing appetite for sensational news, companies and even entire industries were likely to wear a scarlet letter for many years. Stakeholders now demand far more assurance and evidence before declaring that a company has turned around.

Restoring a tarnished corporate reputation now takes closer to four years, while rebuilding a preeminent reputation takes even longer. *Good to Great* esteemed author Jim Collins states that it takes a company ". . . on average four years to crystallize a coherent strategic concept and seven years of intense effort below the radar screen before a company would show a significant and sustained leap to great results."[2] Collins is essentially saying that it takes seven years to go from just *good* to *great*. Reputation recovery—going from *not good* to *just fair,* much less to *great again*—is clearly no small feat.

As the number of companies that suffered corporate crises—and started over to restore their once-good names—continued to mount, I began trying to answer several questions:

- How do companies lose reputation?
- What triggers reputation loss?
- Were there distress signals?
- Why are so many companies struggling with tarnished reputations?
- Who is ultimately responsible for losing reputation?
- What does it take to restore a damaged reputation?
- What can a company do to safeguard its reputation from loss?
- Can a company build an enduring and lasting reputation in this day and age?

Mounting questions such as these were the genesis of this book. I became captivated by this emerging dimension of reputation management—reputation recovery and sustainability—and *Corporate Reputation: 12 Steps to Safeguarding and Recovering Reputation* was born. My interest in the science of recovery is rooted in the belief that everyone deserves the opportunity to redeem themselves and that second-act performances are in many cases far superior to the first.

HOW I WROTE THIS BOOK

When writing *Corporate Reputation*, I relied on Weber Shandwick's landmark reputation recovery research *Safeguarding Reputation*™, performed with KRC Research, and on my past and continuing work as a CEO and corporate reputation counselor. I also used publicly available market research, secondary information, books written by reputation builders, and the extensive offline and online media coverage that follows corporate crises. My overflowing files remained a seemingly limitless source of examples of companies gone amok. They also served as strong sources of inspiration with their equally striking examples of strategies that lifted fallen companies back on their feet.

Having previously written a book on CEO reputation, *CEO Capital: A Guide to Building CEO Reputation and Company Success,*[3] I was already keenly aware of the CEO's role in reputation protection and recovery. On this knowledge, too, I have relied.

THE BOOK'S OBJECTIVES

Overall, *Corporate Reputation* has five objectives that provide the framework for its approach and philosophy:

1. To explain why reputation, more fragile than ever, matters to a company's valuation, well-being, and permission to exist.
2. To isolate a new stage—reputation recovery—that deserves its rightful place in the reputation-building process.
3. To identify the most important steps in recovering reputation.
4. To explain the roles that corporate leaders should play in reputation recovery and sustainability.
5. To provide a road map for restoring reputation over the long term.

THE CONTENT

Corporate Reputation is organized into three parts:

Part I: Chapters 1 through 3 explain why reputation matters, how reputation management is evolving into a top business priority, and what happens when reputation equity is damaged and reputations are lost.

Part II: Chapters 4 through 7 take the reader through the 12 steps of reputation recovery that fall into four phases: Rescue, Rewind, Restore, and Recover. Leaders may spend more time in one phase than another. The steps in the Reputation Recovery model can be reordered and customized to suit the individual, the company, the organization and the situation. Nothing is set in stone. Yet, the steps cannot be ignored.

Part III: Chapter 8 draws conclusions on how to sustain and mend reputations with an evolving and uncertain future ahead.

FOR WHOM THIS BOOK WAS WRITTEN

Corporate Reputation is written primarily for leadership teams, board members, and other professionals such as corporate communications executives, public affairs and marketing officers, risk managers, advertising and public relations firms, executive recruiters, and management consultants. The book also provides guidance for business students, academics, managers, and others who want to understand how great reputations can be destroyed, yet rebuilt by a steady hand, courageous heart, and level head.

CAVEATS

A few caveats are necessary. The companies and leaders mentioned in this book are not necessarily clients, nor have they necessarily sought Weber Shandwick's or anyone else's assistance in safeguarding and rebuilding reputation. All opinions are strictly my own.

As I wrote this book, I drew upon the expertise of my colleagues, interviews, proprietary research, and publicly available information sources. I also applied my own experience and insights, built over more than two decades researching CEO and corporate reputation, and counseling leaders around the world. To those whom I have worked with and who have made these abundant sources available to me, I am immensely grateful. Without them, *Corporate Reputation* could never have been written.

This book is about more than managing a crisis immediately after an incident, disaster, or disclosure. It is not merely about the initial emergency response, the first several hours, or the business continuity services that keep a company up and running when disaster strikes. This book is about the long road back to recovering lost reputation, and preserving an organization and culture that, in many cases, holds an irreplaceable spot in the hearts and minds of employees.

The premise of *Corporate Reputation* is that successful reputation recovery requires more than mere crisis management and more than a focus on that defining moment when disaster strikes. Like the phoenix, the Egyptian mythical bird that set fire to a nest of twigs only to be reborn amidst the ashes, reputations can regenerate themselves; however, this renewal is not a momentary affair. *Corporate Reputation* is not just about what happens in the emergency room, but more about what happens to the patient after the trauma has been diagnosed, lifesaving intervention has been made, vital signs have stabilized, and the patient is out of immediate danger. It is also about postoperative care and the long rehabilitation before a patient can cautiously begin life anew.

REPUTATION LOSS IS NOT NEW, BUT RECOVERY STRATEGIES ARE

The destruction of reputation has been with us for centuries, if not since the beginning of mankind. The Puritans, according to Nathaniel Hawthorne, were no strangers to the damning powers of a fallen reputation. These guardians of religious correctness required that Hester Prynne wear a scarlet "A" to ensure that she would forever bear the reputation of a sinner.

The Enron crisis, the WorldCom debacle, and other corporate break downs amount to modern-day scarlet "A's." These unfortunate events had as damning an effect on corporate standing as the "A" did on Hester Prynne's reputation. There is no reason to believe that similar future crises will be any less damning unless executives first learn to take appropriate, effective, and timely steps to dilute, if not eradicate, the stain of corporate sin.

The carefully run and reputation-conscious company need not remain defenseless when faced with a tarnished reputation. After all, even Hester Prynne was eventually able to counter the effects of her scarlet "A" and by good works "gain . . . from many people the reverence due to an angel."[4] To undertake such good works will take the care and guidance of committed reputation caregivers, steeped in the knowledge of building enduring and lasting reputations.

Leslie Gaines-Ross
Park Slope, Brooklyn
December, 2007

PART I

CHAPTER I

REPUTATION MATTERS

"In today's world, where ideas are increasingly displacing the physical in the production of economic value, competition for reputation becomes a significant driving force, propelling our economy forward."

—Alan Greenspan, former Federal Reserve chairman[1]

"A risk to its reputation is a threat to the survival of the enterprise."

—Peter J. Firestein[2]

A TIPPING POINT

On August 29, 2005, America suffered its biggest disaster since September 11, 2001. Hurricane Katrina hit the north-central Gulf Coast of the United States at 6:10 a.m. with a particularly catastrophic blow to New Orleans. Levees were soon breached, and the South would never be the same.

Thousands of homes were destroyed, leaving tens of thousands of people instantly homeless. As the waters overwhelmed coastal communities, television stations broadcasted dramatic, heart-wrenching images—citizens stranded on roofs waving in desperation to search helicopters, living rooms filled with shattered remains of what were once their homes, and families standing on highways searching for missing loved ones.

Distressing media coverage continued day in and day out, for weeks, and then for months. Even after the waters had long since receded, personal, emotional stories continued to make news. Media accounts of unredeemable flood insurance, undelivered trailers for the homeless, and mounting tales of emotional and physical distress seemed to be never-ending.

The government response at city, state, and federal levels was considered grossly inadequate from the start. Evacuation before and after the hurricane hit was poorly planned and sluggish. Little thought was given to the special needs of the infirm and helpless. Some policemen failed to show up for work. Corpses floated unclaimed amidst the debris in the Lower Ninth Ward. As evacuees squeezed into the Superdome and reports of looting increased at an alarming rate, U.S. President George W. Bush miscalculated the urgency of the crisis and remained vacationing at his Texas ranch.

Several days later, the president visited the suffering port city in a flyover on Air Force One. At an impromptu press conference at the New Orleans airport runway after the flyover, the president praised the head of the Federal Emergency Management Agency (FEMA), Michael Brown. However, Brown would ultimately be the target of more criticism in the coming months than perhaps anyone else involved in Katrina's aftermath. Only as it became increasingly clear that FEMA was unable to provide adequate transportation, food, and shelter did President Bush fire Brown and replace him with an experienced emergency disaster relief admiral.

Two years later, the hard-hit Gulf Coast is still getting back on its feet. Although after-effects of Katrina continue to linger, signs of progress are now visible. Permits and licenses for New Orleans vendors for the 2007 Mardi Gras were up 310 percent from 2006.[3] A Kaiser Family Foundation 2007 study based on New Orleans residents found that some progress was being made in restoring basic services, reopening schools, launching new businesses, and growing its population.[4]

Hurricane Katrina will forever stand as an example of how the American government failed to address one of the country's most serious modern-day catastrophes. Most every American agreed that assistance for Hurricane Katrina victims was received too little, too late. The majority of Americans (58 percent) in a CBS News poll disapproved of the government's handling of relief efforts one week after the hurricane hit.[5] Response to Katrina by the federal government, FEMA, and state and local government was regarded by most Americans as poor (77, 70, and 70 percent, respectively).[6] Equally disturbing, Americans believed that the disaster's response had worsened the already battered overseas image of the United States.[7] Worse still, the American public was left with the impression that the administration's response to the deadly hurricane reflected a lack of compassion and management ability.

Hurricane Katrina had a powerfully negative impact on perceptions of President Bush and his cabinet. The government's missteps served as a negative tipping point for the Bush administration's reputation. Its poor handling of the disaster took on epic proportions and was viewed as intrinsic to the core of the administration's character. Each mistake generated a whole new set of problems. It was not just the administration's failure to anticipate and react in time to the deadly hurricane, but also the magnitude of this failure that led to a material loss in the president's and his administration's reputation.

The traditional rally of support for a president during the aftermath of a national emergency such as the September 11 terrorist attacks was nowhere to be found. Coupled with growing dissatisfaction with the war in Iraq, popular support for the administration reached a point of no return. Unfortunately for President Bush, the administration's past and future actions would thereafter be viewed through the lens of another devastating event.

With no appropriate and effective reputation recovery program for the handling of Hurricane Katrina and the continuing violence in Iraq, the November 2006 midterm Senate, House, and gubernatorial elections were all but preordained. Both houses of Congress gained Democratic majorities, thereby demonstrating just how irreparably damaged the administration's reputation, and that of the political party it represented, had become.

This is not to say that local political issues did not play a role in Hurricane Katrina's devastation. New Orleans Mayor Ray Nagin and Louisiana Governor Kathleen Blanco were both heavily criticized for not ordering New Orleans residents to evacuate early enough. Emergency evacuation plans were implemented less than one day before the hurricane hit, and many people were unable to find safe routes out of the city.

REPUTATION ADVANTAGE

Reputation matters. Reputation means how positively, or negatively, a company or similar institution is perceived by its key stakeholders—the people or entities that the company or institution relies on for its success. For many for-profit companies, typical stakeholders might include customers, employees, suppliers, or financial analysts. For governments or political entities such as the Bush and Blair administrations, stakeholders are, above all, the electorate.

As described in greater detail in the next chapter, reputation loss can strike any company or group. Unfortunately for many companies that have built great reputations, the much-touted adage "the bigger they are, the harder they fall" holds true. Stakeholders can lose confidence in even the most highly admired companies that fail them. Although it may take a catastrophe before stakeholders ultimately lose faith in the great branded companies, it does happen, and then the fall from grace can be fast and furious. Hubris has no place in business. All are susceptible to reputation damage.

If its reputation is strong, a company in crisis is granted the benefit of the doubt by its stakeholders. They expect companies to do the right thing. Even when inevitable mistakes are committed, stakeholders will afford highly regarded companies an additional opportunity to make amends—an opportunity they are not likely to grant the less regarded. When stakeholders view companies in a positive light, they give companies license to continue to operate and grow.

Reputation also contributes directly to a company's health by providing competitive advantage and differentiation. When stakeholders hold a company in high regard, they generate sales by recommending or buying its products/services. They support its ability to invest and grow by recommending or buying its stock. Stakeholders who hold a company in high esteem are more likely to recommend the company as a good place to work, allowing it to attract, develop, and keep the best employees. Those who admire companies spread positive word-of-mouth across a wide social network.

Companies burdened by a tainted reputation have less opportunity to continue business as usual, which further hampers their reputation-comeback efforts. Steps that would otherwise be viewed with optimism, or at least equanimity, are viewed with suspicion and doubt.

Good reputations do more than raise capital and attract the best talent. Admired companies generate additional sales from loyal customers, attract the right strategic and business partners, assure the public that the company will behave ethically, provide a buffer when problems arise, and sometimes permit companies to charge premium prices. Not to be ignored in this age of regulatory watchdogs is how a positive reputation reduces friction with government officials and legislators.

For these reasons and more, there are very real, tangible, "hard" payoffs to maintaining a good reputation. Weber Shandwick's *Safe-guarding Reputation*[TM] research found that a hefty 63 percent of a company's market value is attributable to reputation, according to global business influencers.[8] Executives in all regions of the world agreed with this high valuation. The average compound shareholder returns of the top 10 2006 *Fortune* Most Admired Companies substantially exceeds that of Standard & Poor's (S&P) 500 companies over five- and one-year periods (see Exhibit 1.1). A Pennsylvania State University survey also found that reputable companies from 1983 to 1997 provided considerably better returns on investment compared to the S&P 500—22 percent versus 16 percent, respectively.[9] Reputation is clearly a quantifiable asset and a proven wealth generator.

Good reputation yields "soft" payoffs as well. Companies report that after being named as a "best company to work for," resumes pour in. A leading economist estimated that companies included on the *Working*

EXHIBIT **1.1** *Good Reputations Pay*

Top 10 Fortune *America's Most Admired Companies*	*2003–2006*	*2001–2006*
General Electric	9.2%	1.2%
Starbucks	28.8	30.0
Toyota Motor	18.4	20.8
Berkshire Hathaway	9.3	7.8
Southwest Airlines	−1.6	−3.6
FedEx	17.6	16.3
Apple	99.6	50.6
Johnson & Johnson	10.8	4.2
Procter & Gamble	11.0	12.5
Goldman Sachs	27.6	17.5
Top 10 Average	23.1	15.7
Top 10 Median	14.3	14.4
S&P 500	10.4	6.2

The 2006 survey findings were reported in the March 19, 2007, issue of *Fortune*.
  Compound annual return.
Notes: To exclude currency effects, Toyota's returns are calculated from yen data.
  Google ranked eighth, but three- and five-year returns were unavailable, as Google went
  public on August 18, 2004.

Mother "100 Best Companies for Working Mothers" list are worth 3 to 6 percent more than their peers that did not make the list.[10] As *Workforce* magazine wrote: "The effort doesn't always pay off in a high ranking, but a high ranking always pays off in invigorating a company's reputation among recruits, employees, shareholders, investors, and customers."[11] Making *Fortune*'s Best Places to Work list opens wide the recruiting door, as financial services giant Edward Jones found out—job applications went from 7,000 to 400,000 one year after landing on the list.[12]

In sharp contrast to the multiple payoffs of good reputation are the real costs of a poor reputation. Least-admired 2006 *Fortune* Most Admired Companies perform considerably worse than the average S&P500 company.[13] These numbers are not surprising since the reason for a poor reputation may be due to a company's poor financial performance. But it is also true that a poor reputation may be part of a vicious cycle. Poorly regarded companies have a hard time attracting talent, new business, new partnerships, referrals, customers, and higher pricing compared to highly regarded companies. Companies that suffer from reputation failure have to work harder and longer than companies held in high esteem.

As Hurricane Katrina tragically demonstrated, losing reputation is a defining moment for a company, country, institution, or individual. Benjamin Franklin once advised that "glass, china, and reputation are easily cracked, and never well mended." Franklin was only partially correct. Yes, reputations are inherently fragile and can tumble without warning overnight. However, the repair process has greatly improved since the eighteenth century. Today, companies can expect to do more than merely patch a tattered reputation back together. As this book demonstrates, rebuilding a strong reputation is well within the realm of possibility. If the right steps are taken, reputation restoration is likely.

CHAPTER 2

REPUTATION LOSS

"It's like we went through this valley of death."

—Jim Allchin, co-president, Microsoft Platforms
and Services Division 2003[1]

"If you lose dollars for the firm by bad decisions, I will be understanding.
If you lose reputation for the firm, I will be ruthless."

—Attributed to Warren Buffett, chairman, Berkshire Hathaway

REPUTATION EROSION

For years, Wal-Mart was one of America's great business success stories.
Sam Walton, a young man from Arkansas and a David among Goliaths,
made it big time. Not only did he compete successfully against the giant
chain stores run by well-heeled, high-born East Coast management types,
but Walton overwhelmingly dominated them by using all-American
values of thrift, industry, and ingenuity.

From a single neighborhood variety store in Rogers, Arkansas, in
1962, Sam Walton created a mega-industry with over 6,500 stores
spanning 15 countries and earning gross revenues in excess of $312
billion in 2006. Wal-Mart became one of America's biggest employers
with nearly two million employees.[2] In 2003, *Fortune* chose Wal-Mart

as America's most admired retailer.[3] Horatio Alger never had it so good.

Much has changed since 2003. Although still a financial powerhouse admired throughout the world, Wal-Mart is no longer the darling of America. Allegations of low wages and inadequate employee health care coverage have taken a toll on the brand, changing Wal-Mart's reputation from the folksy, low-price champion to that of the besieged discount behemoth.

This sudden reputation turnaround seriously took root in 2005 when the first national survey by Zogby International[4] found that the American public had an increasingly poor view of Wal-Mart despite the company's claim that it had saved consumers $263 billion in 2004 alone.[5] The poll also reported that nearly 4 in 10 Americans held an unfavorable opinion of Wal-Mart and more than 5 in 10 believed that Wal-Mart's public image would get worse. According to the Zogby poll, 56 percent of Americans agreed with the damning statement: "Wal-Mart [is] bad for America. It may provide low prices, but these prices come with a high moral and economic cost." The once legendary and revered Wal-Mart, founded by the down-home Sam Walton, had clearly lost its Midas touch.

Fortune 500 giants such as Henry Ford, Thomas Watson, and Sam Walton might have all agreed that the "business of business is business." That was then. Today, companies are judged on more than financial performance and physical assets. A company's value increasingly depends on management's ability to manage its intangible assets such as ideas, knowledge, expertise, talent, leadership, customer service, and *reputation*. These intangibles can now comprise up to 70 percent of a company's market capitalization.[6] In fact, the intangible value of many companies today can exceed their tangible value. For an iconic company such as Coca-Cola, the majority of its market capitalization is accounted for by its brand.[7] Intangibles such as reputation lie at the heart of business today.

With companies now unable to afford to overlook any competitive advantage, an intangible asset such as reputation matters more than ever. To be concerned with business is to be concerned with reputation.

The majority of CEOs worldwide now believe that reputation matters more than it did several years ago. CEOs, chairmen, and senior board members are more likely to spontaneously mention reputation as a factor in measuring company worth. This estimation of reputation as a measure of corporate wealth often outranks financial performance and product/ service quality. Relative to 1983, only 8 percent of business leaders mentioned reputation as a significant component in their company valuation.[8]

Once seemingly impregnable, corporate reputations have fallen suddenly and precipitously. The last decade has seen many of the world's most admired companies descend from their once lofty perches. These companies had been in a class by themselves—corporate reputation royalty whose invincibility was universally accepted by business executives and the media around the globe. No one would have predicted that they would ever part with their crowns. Yet they were dethroned.

Consider these extraordinary facts about several legendary Fortune 500 companies:

- Only three companies from *Fortune's* America's Top 10 Most Admired Companies in 2000 were among the Top 10 Most Admired in 2006.
- Once ranked number 1 in *Fortune's* America's Most Admired Companies survey, technology behemoth IBM fell to rank number 354 in 1993. Ten years later, IBM made it back into the *Fortune* Top 10 America's Most Admired All-Star list and now ranks at the top of its industry.
- Sony, a one-time high-flier in the corporate reputation league tables, now ranks sixth in its industry in the *Fortune* 2006 World's Most Admired Companies survey. Just three years ago, it ranked second in its industry.

Reputation failure is no longer a threat that looms large for companies only in high-risk industries and activities. It has become an all-too-familiar scenario for all companies in all corners of the world. A Weber Shandwick proprietary analysis revealed that 33 percent of the 2005

Global *Fortune* 500—the world's largest companies—experienced reputation deterioration in their "most-admired" status from the previous year. The reputations of the remaining 67 percent stayed the same or improved.

Reputation loss is also on the rise. Nearly 9 out of 10 business executives participating in Weber Shandwick's *Safeguarding Reputation*™ survey agree that susceptibility to reputation damage is a growing threat.[9] Similarly, a sizable 84 percent of global senior executives surveyed by the Economist Intelligence Unit (EIU) reported that reputation risk increased significantly over the past five years. When executives were asked to choose among 13 risk types, reputation risk emerged as the most significant threat to global corporate business. As seen in Exhibit 2.1, reputation risk exceeded all others, including regulatory risk, human capital risk, information technology (IT) network risk, and market risk. Reputation risk was considered even more threatening than terrorism, natural hazards, and physical security.[10]

EXHIBIT **2.1** *Greatest Business Risks*

Reputation risk	52
Regulatory risk	41
Human capital risks	41
IT network risk	35
Market risk	32
Credit risk	29
Country risk	22
Financing risk	21
Terrorism	19
Foreign exchange risk	18
Natural hazard risk	18
Political risk	18
Crime	15

Note: that figures are indexed.
Source: Economist Intelligence Unit, "Reputation: Risk of Risks," 2005.

EXHIBIT **2.2** *Hardest Phase of Reputation Management*

	Total Executives	North America	Europe	Asia
Building reputation	10%	9%	11%	9%
Maintaining reputation	24	19	25	25
Recovering reputation	66	72	64	66

Note: Results for Brazilian executives are included in the total.
Source: Weber Shandwick *Safeguarding Reputation*™ with KRC Research, 2006.

Unfortunately, losing reputation is now considered to be an inevitable by-product of usual business operations. If a company is in business long enough, it will at some point lose reputation and will have to know how to respond. Weber Shandwick's survey[11] found that approximately one-third (31 percent) of global business leaders believe that their companies will likely sustain reputation damage in the next two years.

Not only are reputation failures perceived to be commonplace, but a solid majority of global business executives (66 percent) believe that recovering reputation is much harder than building or maintaining reputation (see Exhibit 2.2). Many executives in the EIU survey (62 percent) concurred. They agreed that managing reputation risk was harder to manage than other risk.

THE NEW REPUTATION RULES OF ENGAGEMENT

Why have the good names of seemingly invincible companies—once deemed as stable as the Rock of Gibraltar—become so vulnerable? Times have changed and changed quickly, requiring a dramatic reexamination of reputation failure.

Three key factors underlie the increasing vulnerability of corporate reputation:

1. Information Revolution
2. Influential Microconstituencies
3. Public Trust

Traditional reputation management required rapt attention to how a company was perceived, narrowing the gap between perception and reality, identifying competitive advantage, and communicating to select audiences. New reputation management does no less, but also requires relentless attention to budding microtrends and developing rapid-response strategies. Whereas companies once concentrated only on one clearly defined, narrow audience such as the financial community and business media, today's reputation focus is multidimensional. Companies must attend to a diverse and all-powerful portfolio of stakeholders that now include online media, environmental groups, and bloggers that constantly command attention.

Information Revolution

Of all the changes that have altered the reputation landscape, the information revolution is probably the most significant. Technology advances have accelerated the speed of information transmission, expanded the size of audiences who receive information, and introduced an unconventional group of opinion shapers who often play by their own rules. While companies once had considerable discretion over when to issue press releases and retain significant control over what they told customers, employees, or Wall Street, all this is no more. Because of the information revolution, the ever-present media, dissatisfied customers, disgruntled employees, and unhappy investors now wait for no one.

For example, if a parent in Canada discovers a shard of glass in her toddler's food, the news can spread worldwide via a blog or chat room. All this can occur within moments, even before the food company's leadership has had time to draft a written statement and seek legal counsel about the incident.

Whereas reputation control was once in the company's hands, control has now shifted. Power no longer lies solely with the traditional transmitter of information, the corporation, but has switched to the traditional receivers of information, customers and influencers. These new information brokers, unencumbered by policies and procedures, receive and transmit information far more nimbly than any organization could ever hope to do. Companies have no choice but to adapt to being not just initiators but also responders to information in a networked world.

Making matters even more difficult is the complexity that technology has now unleashed on social networks. Multiple sources of information erupt instantaneously via different channels to make information hard for the ordinary person to manage and absorb. In 2003, health analyst David Rothkopf identified a new phenomenon when analyzing the severe acute respiratory syndrome (SARS) crisis. Describing how reports of SARS initiated worldwide hysteria, Rothkopf termed such technological diffusion of information among multiple and varied pathways as information epidemics or *infodemics*.[12]

> An infodemic is not the rapid spread of simple news via the media, nor is it simply the rumor mill on steroids. Rather, as with SARS, it is a complex phenomenon caused by the interaction of mainstream media, specialist media and internet sites; and "informal" media, which is to say wireless phones, text messaging, pagers, faxes and e-mail, all transmitting some combination of fact, rumor, interpretation and propaganda. It can be rendered more difficult to understand by multiple languages, cultures and attitudes toward the free and open flow of information.[13]

These infodemics spread, as was the case in China, by a lack of prompt and credible disclosure by the targeted organization and the failure to adopt timely, responsive countersteps.

Rothkopf describes infodemics as analogous to health epidemics in that they are virulent and a threat to societal and business functioning, and have well-known carriers. In the case of SARS, the ensuing infodemic led to an exceedingly high, unnecessarily incurred economic cost: airlines, tourism, and exports stalled, and several Asian economies were shattered. Rothkopf's cure for treating such infodemics squares with taming reputation panics—earned credibility. If Chinese health officials had shared more information earlier and been less secretive, and in the process bolstered their reputation, the SARS epidemic might not have spread as far and wide as it did. As the saying goes, sunlight is the best disinfectant.

Damning information, however, need not rise to the level of an infodemic to have adverse consequences. The new information revolution has the unfortunate effect of vesting even mere rumor with the power of truth. Rumors are less fatal than infodemics but can nevertheless unleash considerable havoc on a company's reputation and bottom line.

The Internet has spawned a new breed of critics and reputation assassins. Armed with little more than a computer and an opinion, these chat-room transmitters and bloggers can undo a company's reputation by disseminating misinformation and innuendo. Such rumors, however, can be countered, at least in part, by truth. For this reason, the Coca-Cola Company designates an area on its corporate web site titled "Myths and Rumors." Credible information, promptly posted, can help Coca-Cola quickly put to bed all rumors and debunk hearsay about a range of topics—the beverage company's ingredients ("Saccharin does not cause cancer"), the Middle East ("Coca-Cola does not contain materials unsuitable for vegetarians and Muslims"), and its products ("Soft drinks do not cause kidney failure").[14]

The information revolution is not all negative. Companies can and do use the Internet to build strong reputations. In 2004, the once high-flying Burger King had been suffering from poor management, lack of oversight, and shrinking market share. McDonald's and Wendy's success seemed to quash any hope of Burger King's resurgence. Burger King was fast becoming irrelevant to its highly desirable young-adult target audience. To distinguish itself from its family-friendly competitors, the fast-food chain had to distinguish itself by being edgier and hipper.

Its reputation boost arrived in the form of Subservient Chicken, an interactive web site promotion (www.subservientchicken.com) that featured a chicken-suited man responding to visitors' commands. This unusual, viral-fueled online marketing promotion for its new Tender-Crisp chicken sandwiches was a runaway success. Nearly eight million daily visitors to Burger King's site jump-started the company's rebranding among twenty-somethings and earned the chain a place on popular sought-after brands-to-watch lists.

The information revolution is clearly a double-edged sword. It presents opportunities for, as well as barriers to, recovering lost reputation or boosting a languishing reputation. On the one hand, the Internet allows an unfavorable problem or issue to remain before the public interminably. On the other hand, the Internet enhances a company's ability to rectify the very same problem or issue by transmitting its rebuttal just as widely, just as rapidly, and just as clearly. If harnessed properly, technology has the potential to effectively air company points of view and quickly counter negative perceptions. The Internet affords a company the opportunity to nip a problem in the bud before it explodes and prepare stakeholders before any damage is done. The Internet's charm and cruelty have transformed how companies protect and recover reputations forever.

Influential Microconstituencies

The rise of small but powerful audiences has forever changed the global economic, societal, and political landscape, including reputation management. Whereas size used to be all that mattered, influential audiences as small as one can now deflate a company, institution, or individual reputation. New microconstituencies begun with meager funds surface every day and shape how companies operate, treat employees, manage the environment, outsource goods, and contribute to society. Many mini-coalitions are single-issue focused, with a mandate to criticize and shame organizations in the hope of changing their corporate behavior.

Microconstituencies can range from individual whistle-blowers (e.g., Sherron Watkins of Enron) and nongovernmental organizations (NGOs) (e.g., Greenpeace and PETA [People for the Ethical Treatment of Animals]) to anticompany sites (e.g., starbucked.com and walmartwatch.com), loose confederations of like-minded people (e.g., car enthusiasts and vegetarians), and class-action plaintiffs and litigators (e.g., www.vioxxlegalresources.com and www.hurtbyabaddrug.com). Although not all deserve labels such as reputation bandits and Robin

Hoods, these groups all have the potential to undermine reputations and plant doubt in customers' and other audiences' minds as to a company's integrity, purpose and practices, and quality of products and services.

One such empowered activist is arch Shell critic Alfred Donovan.[15] No one was more surprised than Royal Dutch Shell PLC to learn that this 88-year-old British army veteran had purchased the Internet domain name www.royaldutchshellplc.com. The gadfly Donovan was a well-known, though underestimated, critic of the company. By acquiring the domain name, Donovan obtained the perfect platform to voice his criticisms of the oil giant. Who would have thought a decade ago that such an unlikely individual could stand up to a corporate powerhouse, waging a war of words against one of the world's largest companies?

Michael Moore, another example of an individual activist, exemplifies the new twenty-first-century microinfluencer. Moore rode to fame by taking on major organizations such as General Motors (*Roger & Me*), the gun lobby (*Bowling for Columbine*), and the health care industry (*SiCKO*). Moore's actions have caused some of the largest pharmaceutical companies to issue Moore *alerts*, advising employees not to speak to the filmmaker, less their remarks be used against them and their companies.

Moore's veracity has been challenged. His tendency to take a kernel of truth and then expand on it for dramatic effect to create a powerful propaganda tract has been criticized by some. As Slate.com columnist Christopher Hitchens summed up Moore's earlier film about President George W. Bush: "*Fahrenheit 9/11* is a sinister exercise in moral frivolity, crudely disguised as an exercise in seriousness."[16] As *SiCKO* was being released in May 2007, Canadian documentarian Debbie Melnyk criticized Moore: "Michael knows the entertainment quotient trumps all."[17] Be that as it may, Moore's influence on public opinion cannot be denied.

Whether Moore ethically abides by a fair portrayal of the facts or not is beside the point. The Oscar-winning filmmaker's influence and scope has grown exponentially. In early 2005, Moore's *Fahrenheit 9/11* won best movie of the year by 21 million people voting in the People's Choice

Awards. The film also won best picture at the 2004 Cannes Film Festival. His films about corporate failings have drawn, and undoubtedly will continue to draw, mass audiences. It would be nearsighted not to see the extraordinary success of this party of one.

The blogosphere is yet another avenue through which the growing pool of microconstituencies may exercise influence. During the 2004 presidential election, CBS's reputation was seriously undermined after veteran anchor Dan Rather alleged that President George W. Bush had received special treatment during his stint in the Texas Air National Guard. Matthew and Greg Sheffeld's conservative blog— www.RatherBiased.com—fueled other bloggers' assault on Rather's broadcast. Over 500,000 people visited their site,[18] resulting in intensive scrutiny of CBS's evidence for the Rather allegation and ultimately forcing an apology ("mistake in judgment"). A few months later, the veteran newscaster retired after more than four decades. His reputation and that of CBS was seriously compromised.

Once again, it is important to underscore that not all activists are reputation mavericks who are always throwing stones at corporations. In fact, Greenpeace USA Executive Director John Passacantando recommends that when companies are under attack they should call these new influentials directly and ask to tell their side of the story off the record.[19] True, they can unfairly harm reputations and place doubt in customers' minds as to a company's credibility. But they can also serve as corporate watchdogs that keep company behavior in check and elicit greater responsibility from an often tunnel-visioned business community that might easily overlook crucial matters or ignore moral propriety. In a new age of corporate transparency, microconstituencies are part of a new equation of checks and balances that companies must now take into consideration when acting. They serve a valuable purpose and should not—must not—be ignored.

According to an EIU survey among global senior executives, companies spend little or no time monitoring perceptions of microconstituencies such as political activists, pressure groups, and local NGOs. Incredibly, only 3 percent of companies monitor international NGOs.[20] This is true even though transnational NGOs are among the few entities in a position to counter transnational companies.

Yet these groups are often underestimated. Despite the proliferation of these microconstituencies and their many successes, corporate leaders are still often caught unprepared when faced with their tenacious opposition to corporate policies. Leaders are often loath to acknowledge the explosive power that these microconstituencies command in current business affairs. Like it or not, these organizations have taken root in the business landscape and will continue to thrive in the years ahead.

Microconstituencies, both national and international, are a new set of influencers that have overturned traditional ways of managing reputation nearly overnight.

Public Trust

As the financial services industry faced one scandal after another in 2002 and 2003, then–Citigroup Chairman Sandy Weill insightfully speculated: "Just imagine how the events of the last year look to that man or woman in the street."[21] Weill hit the nail on the head. The general public was not impressed by these scandals. Citizens were rapidly losing faith in business.

Is it important for companies to win the public's approval and trust? Absolutely. As Arthur W. Page, namesake of the well-respected member organization for senior public relations and corporate communications officers, said many years ago: "All business begins with the public permission and exists by public approval, and roughly speaking, the more approval you have, the better you live."[22]

The public is now a genuine economic force, accustomed to expressing its likes and dislikes through individual or group action. Today, many people routinely express themselves with their pocketbooks by not buying gas-guzzling cars, ordering only fair-trade coffee, and avoiding movies they consider morally unacceptable. The public has become increasingly effective and well organized in voicing their opinions. For example, Nike products faced massive boycotts years ago due to the perception that they were mistreating third-world employees.

Even small local communities can successfully pressure companies to change broad policies, and contribute financially or volunteer employees to important community causes. Research by Weber Shandwick underscores an increasing societal advocacy and faster speed to action on behalf of companies and their products, issues, and causes.[23]

Civil society is no longer a passive group whose sole purpose is to serve as a mass market for company products and services. According to Opinion Leader Research analysts Deborah Mattinson and Graeme Trayner, companies and organizations now face not only aggressive media but an assertive public.[24] The researchers rightfully state: "In a world where 51 of the 100 largest economic entities are companies rather than countries, people have become aware of the power of business. Companies are judged on factors such as 'corporate citizenship', and are perceived to have wider obligations beyond profit and shareholder return."[25]

Due to lingering mistrust resulting from past and present corporate scandals, the public now demands that companies justify their actions. According to pollster MORI, three out of four members of the British public say they would believe an employee over company advertising or marketing when it comes to corporate citizenship.[26] For a company to gain the public's trust, it is not just a charitable act or even a "politically correct" move. Making sure that the public is on the company's side is good business.

To monitor the mounting influence of public opinion, Opinion Leader Research advises companies to adopt "permanent campaigns." They counsel companies to adopt many of the practices of political parties. Companies should consider the public as voters, not just consumers. They should think of the public as an electorate with whom they must constantly create and foster relationships. They must actively campaign for the public's support to protect their reputations and to earn, as Arthur Page says, their licenses to operate.

Companies continue to do just that. In 2003, the *New York Times* suffered a decline in reputation when star reporter Jayson Blair was found to have fabricated the sources of several articles. In an attempt to repair its reputation as the premier member of the fourth estate, *Times* editors created the "Public Editor," an ombudsman to represent the *Times* readership. The public editor is typically a journalist with no prior *Times* relationship who is charged with following up on reader complaints. The public editor was given the authority to conduct an independent investigation and report on investigation findings in a weekly column for all to read. By regularly and actively engaging its more vocal populace, companies such as the *New York Times* stand a better chance of sustaining their reputations over the long-term.

Reputation loss can be hard to quantify. However, when it is fading or absent, companies and the people who work for them can feel it. Making sure that the telltale signs of eroding reputation are noticed is the work of leaders.

CHAPTER 3

SECOND ACTS

"Reputation is an account in credit with our customers and stake-holders. The balance can be drawn down as well as augmented."

—Phil Watts, former chairman, Royal Dutch Shell[1]

"Ice storm's coming tomorrow everybody. Ice storm's coming. How do we make sure this never happens again? And I'm convinced if it happened tomorrow, we would be maybe as good as we have been in the past on snowstorms. But I am convinced if it happens two weeks from now that we're going to be 10 times better than we've ever been. And if it happens, let's see, April 1, it's going to be amazing how we'll be able to deal with it."

—David Neeleman, JetBlue's former CEO, in response to his airline's February 2007 flight cancellations[2]

REPUTATION RISING

As discussed in Chapter 2, Wal-Mart, one of America's most revered companies, is struggling to right its reputation. Several years earlier, another one of America's most admired companies, the famed Xerox Company, suffered a similar reputation challenge. Xerox's reputation loss was not due to shifting public expectations, as was the case with Wal-Mart, but to more typical business reasons such as mismanagement and business losses. Although Wal-Mart's efforts to recover its good name appear headed in the right direction, Xerox's reputation recovery has already been hailed as an unqualified success. Xerox currently boasts a sterling reputation that is as good as, if not better than, the proud one of years past. The turnaround is largely due to the colossal efforts of its Chief Executive Anne Mulcahy.

When Mulcahy was handed the reins in 2001, Xerox was over $17 billion in debt and holding less than $155 million in available cash. Its stock price had plunged from nearly $64 to under $5. Lost market share, negligence, a U.S. Securities and Exchange Commission (SEC) accounting investigation, and near bankruptcy were just a few of its many problems. The *Fortune* 500 company was in free fall. Making matters worse, the company chose an untested CEO to save it. When Mulcahy was named CEO-elect, Xerox's stock dropped 15 percent. She took over during its darkest hour. Even Mulcahy had to agree that Xerox's business model was unsustainable.

How did this first-time CEO turn the company around? Her first order of business was to earn credibility for herself and Xerox by showing early signs of progress. This she accomplished by focusing on financial stability, quickly selling unprofitable business units, and accelerating retirements. Then Mulcahy took several critical steps to begin refurbishing Xerox's tarnished reputation—she was brutally honest about problems; asked for help; communicated tirelessly; listened carefully; established clear priorities; retained only the best of its corporate culture; built her team; and made firm, tough calls. Having taken these steps, Mulcahy then focused the organization on three main goals—reducing $1 billion in costs, selling $2 billion in assets, and concentrating on the core business.

Five years later, the Xerox turnaround was undeniable. As Mulcahy said, "In many ways, the curtain has closed on the Xerox turnaround. But we are keenly aware that most great plays have two acts."[3] While the curtain goes up on Xerox's second act, the document company's reputation is mended—but only for the time being. Mulcahy wisely pointed out that reputation restoration is never complete. When done correctly, restoring reputation is always a work in progress. Reputations are always vulnerable to change. A company must always strive to meet ever-higher standards, always protecting its reputation. According to Mulcahy, Xerox must be more than good enough: "We constantly remind ourselves that the enemy of great is good."[4] The curtain rises and falls on a company every night, and every night is a new act.

The lessons learned by Anne Mulcahy when turning around Xerox include many of the steps discussed in this book. But the most important lesson to be learned is that by taking appropriate steps, recovery is not only possible but indeed likely. Despite deep concern over any loss to reputation, the vast majority of global business decision makers believe that companies can recover reputation. Weber Shandwick's *Safeguarding Reputation*™ research found that 91 percent of global executives report that tarnished reputations can be restored.[5]

Luckily, not many global *Fortune 500* companies go out of business because a crisis struck or a damaging issue surfaced. Spectacular dis-integrations like that which befell Arthur Andersen are exceptions. Most large companies that lose reputation have the opportunity, resources, and residual goodwill to recast their companies with new CEOs, new boards, new partners, and new visions, as did Tyco, WorldCom, CA, AIG, Royal Ahold, Parmalat, Skandia, and Vivendi, to name just a few. For big players such as these, the issue is usually not so much a question of whether recovery will happen, but more a question of how soon recovery will take place and whether recovery will return the company to its former reputational glory.

Decades need not pass before lost reputations are restored. Business decision makers estimate that, when recovery is properly managed, approximately three and a half years are required for a company to rebuild its damaged reputation.[6] This figure squares with the assessment of former Chairman and CEO Louis Gerstner when he declared that IBM's reputation recovery that began in 1993 was completed by 1997—a four-year recovery period.[7]

Some leaders might flinch at the thought of facing impatient and often judgmental boards, shareholders, analysts, journalists, customers, and employees for as long as four years. Restoring reputation, however, is not a 1-2-3 fix. Reputation may be lost in a flash, but recovery takes time. Once stakeholders view a reputation as having been seriously diminished, pessimism sets in. Stakeholders cling to a negativism that takes time to overcome. For example, while Cisco Systems was highly touted in the late 1990s as the tech wunderkind, people were quick to enumerate its failings when its financial performance slipped during the dot-com industry implosion. As earlier noted, Xerox did not recover its reputation immediately or even soon afterward. It took Xerox five years, and might have taken much longer had its recovery not been so expertly managed.

A silver lining, however, often graces even the darkest of storm clouds. This is what Mulcahy discovered when she began cleaning house at Xerox. She was free to challenge long-held assumptions and impose substantive transformations that under more positive circumstances would never have been possible or tolerated. In this sense, reputation loss is analogous to the forest fire that allows a new, fresh, and stronger forest to grow where rotted, tangled trees once stood. Freed of the weeds, brush, and dead wood that have accumulated over time, the new forest can now flourish unimpeded. While business leaders are unlikely to invite a crisis so that they can start fresh and anew, nearly all confirm that losing reputation provides a once-in-a-lifetime opportunity to make things better. Obviously, reputation loss is to be avoided, but should it occur, the follow-up effort to recover reputation constitutes a universally recognized opportunity to initiate sorely needed change.

ONE STEP AT A TIME

This book provides a step-by-step guide to protecting and recovering reputation. Its pages present steps that have been culled from the best practices of companies spanning regions and industries. As the twenty-first century unfolds, there is no shortage of companies and executives whose attempts at reputation recovery cannot be observed. Hewlett-Packard, Morgan Stanley, Dell, the *New York Times*, Disney, Airbus, Sony, JetBlue,

EXHIBIT **3.1** *12 Steps to Safeguarding and Recovering Reputation*

Stage One:	**Rescue**
Step 1:	Take the Heat—Leader First
Step 2:	Communicate Tirelessly
Step 3:	Reset the Company Clock
Step 4:	Don't Underestimate Your Critics and Competitors
Stage Two:	**Rewind**
Step 5:	Analyze What Went Wrong *and* Right
Step 6:	Measure, Measure, and Measure Again
Stage Three:	**Restore**
Step 7:	Right the Culture
Step 8:	Seize the Shift
Step 9:	Brave the Media
Stage Four:	**Recover**
Step 10:	Build a Drumbeat of Good News
Step 11:	Commit to a Marathon, Not a Sprint
Step 12:	Minimize Reputation Risk

LiveDoor, NTT, Gap, Royal Dutch Shell, General Motors, Nissan, and Ford are merely the blue-chip tip of an iceberg that conceals an increasing number of corporations, organizations, and institutions that have and will face the challenge of recovering reputation.

Twelve steps fit into a four-stage reputation recovery model as outlined in Exhibit 3.1—Stage One: Rescue (minimizing the damage); Stage Two: Rewind (identifying what went wrong); Stage Three: Restore (rebuilding reputation); and Stage Four: Recover (sustaining reputation for the long term).

Before moving on to a discussion of each step in the chapters ahead, the roles to be played by the CEO and board of directors should be noted. Their participation in safeguarding and repairing reputation has changed markedly in recent years.

CEO as Chief Reputation Officer

Years ago, the position of reputation manager resided several levels below the CEO. For the most part, building reputation was equated with image building. Advertising to mass audiences was the remedy. CEOs might sign off on agency budgets when advertising was about to launch or ask where commercials were running. Today's CEOs are actively involved in all aspects of how the company is portrayed. They want to participate in selecting the marketing communications company, brainstorm ideas, approve online and offline media channels, identify opinion leaders, wordsmith press releases, and handpick speaking opportunities at executive conferences and university forums. Twenty-first-century leaders recognize that reputation is much more than clever campaign pledges, sharp advertising, and catchy taglines.

The final say on reputation management today belongs to the chief executive. CEOs now realize that reputation management is as important and complex as any other high-level business function. As GE CEO Jeff Immelt said, "My own role on the GE board is clear. I have two functions: lead the company as CEO with integrity, clarity and purpose, as measured by financial performance and reputation; lead the board as chairman with vision and openness. . . . "[8] CEO involvement in reputation building and management is now a strategic line job, not just window dressing.

Furthermore, as discussed in my earlier book, *CEO Capital: A Guide to Building CEO Reputation and Company Success*,[9] CEO reputation is inextricably linked to company reputation. When the CEO speaks, the company speaks. The CEO is the face of the company. Accordingly, the CEO must ensure that the manner in which she presents herself to stakeholders—whether it is customers, Wall Street, or employees—must be consistent with the company's vision, code of conduct, and values.

The CEO is also the strategic player in reputation recovery. Strategic advisers Rory Knight and Deborah Pretty have examined the relationship between leadership and reputation recovery. Their firm, Oxford Metrica, concluded that crises are times when CEOs can build reputation equity and value for their company. Knight and Pretty's in-depth analysis of recovering and nonrecovering firms found that as alter egos of the company, CEOs must demonstrate specific qualities and behavior: "Honesty, transparency and effective communication have a clear and fundamental financial value. Relevant and timely information must be given: management must respond honestly and rapidly in a nondefensive way."[10] Essentially, a CEO's ability to manage reputational difficulties is the determining factor in whether stakeholders retain confidence in the company and believe that reputation will eventually be restored.

For this reason, failure to maintain reputation rests squarely on the CEO's shoulders. *Safeguarding Reputation*™ found that when crisis strikes, nearly 60 percent of the responsibility for the crisis is attributed to the CEO.[11] Additionally, an Economist Intelligence Unit (EIU) survey on reputation risk found that the vast majority of global senior executives (84 percent) identify the CEO as reputation bearer twice as often as the board of directors (42 percent).[12]

CEOs themselves feel no differently. Most CEOs would agree that reputation management responsibility primarily lies at their door. Other department heads such as marketing—the department traditionally responsible for advertising—barely figure into the reputation equation. As former GE Chairman and CEO Jack Welch wrote: "Image mattered. I was convinced it was my job."[13]

Although reputation erosion is usually the result of more than one person's failure, the loss is rarely shared. In some cases it can reach the senior management team; however, the blame for reputation loss usually lands at the threshold of the CEO's office door. When reputations fail, current CEOs are typically ousted, and new CEOs are ushered in and held responsible for cleaning up the damage and returning the company to its former glory. Failing to safeguard reputation at a time when reputations are so volatile is possibly one reason why CEO turnover rates worldwide are so high.[14]

Heightened Board Responsibility

Despite greater board oversight since the Sarbanes-Oxley Act of 2002, boards are held less responsible than CEOs for reputation mismanagement. Indications exist, however, that board responsibility for reputation failure is increasing. As board members find themselves personally liable, directors are asking hard-hitting questions. As corporate governance expert Charles Elson sums up board member risks, "Your wealth is at stake, and your reputation is at stake."[15] To great embarrassment, individual board members are now publicly named and shamed when companies fail to perform. In some cases, directors are required to pay millions of dollars out of their own pockets to settle shareholder lawsuits alleging poor governance.

The New York Stock Exchange's board members were publicly vilified for having approved $139.5 million in deferred compensation for dismissed Chairman Dick Grasso. Several board members subsequently resigned as well. When it comes to board reputation, Hewlett-Packard's board was slammed hard in 2006 when the public learned that its chairman and other senior officers authorized gathering information under false pretenses in an attempt to discover media leaks. These days, board members have to worry about their reputations and, by extension, the reputations of their own companies.

New governmental regulations and shareholder advocates now demand that boards provide greater oversight when things go awry. Board members increasingly recognize that they need to stay involved because company reputation is always at stake, even as a company performs its most mundane operations. Many would agree that they should take on more aggressive and active roles when companies face ethical challenges. When serious financial problems arose at mortgage lender New Century Financial Corporation, board members became more involved and lent their years of crisis experience to the fairly new CEO.[16] Boards are no longer disengaged and immune when reputations are in harm's way.

Selecting the right CEO for complex and uncertain times is among a board's most critical roles. Whereas most outgoing CEOs once practically handpicked heirs, most boards now play very active roles in evaluating and selecting CEO candidates. The Walt Disney Company's board, for example, thought long and hard about choosing a replacement for infamous CEO Michael Eisner. The board eventually chose insider Robert Iger over highly respected outsider eBay CEO Meg Whitman, among others. Disney's reputation had been spiraling downhill as management ranks thinned and the company faced unprecedented shareholder criticism of Eisner's management style. In an effort to build confidence, Disney Board Chairman, and former Senator George Mitchell, publicly announced on March 13, 2005, the unanimous election of Robert Iger as chief executive officer. In explicit detail, the board laid out each step in the selection process:

- We have done everything we said we would do.
- All non-management directors were fully and actively engaged in the process. Bob Iger recused himself from the process, and the Board consulted with Michael Eisner as appropriate.
- We selected the executive search firm of Heidrick & Struggles.
- We carefully considered an internal and several external candidates. We evaluated a large number of individuals, in consultation with Heidrick & Struggles, and board members met with potential candidates.
- Since we began the process last September, the board has devoted 11 meetings to this subject; including 9 in-person meetings, one video conference, and one telephonic meeting. During those meetings, the board covered the subject in the most detailed and careful manner.
- During its 11 meetings on succession, the board regularly met first with Michael Eisner present and then met for an extended period of time without him present.
- As I said, Bob Iger recused himself and did not participate at all in any of the meetings.
- In addition to selecting a successor, we have developed a plan to achieve a smooth and effective transition.[17]

Years ago, a full and detailed explanation from the board of directors of a company such as Disney would not have been expected. Today's attention to CEO selection, particularly when a company's reputation has been sullied, calls for explicit communications and, as Disney's board demonstrated, transparency.

Reputation damage exacts a tremendous price from a company in terms of profitability, share price, employee attraction and retention, and competitive position. As described in the first three chapters of this book, reputation is too important today to neglect or take for granted.

The next four chapters detail how to protect reputation and take the necessary steps to restore the most valuable and competitive company asset.

PART II

CHAPTER 4

RESCUE

"The only battles you are certain to lose are the ones you don't fight."

—Carlos Ghosn, Nissan CEO during its turnaround[1]

"The oil has been cleaned up, leaving behind a bare two-acre patch of ground, but the leak—and the subsequent discovery that six miles of BP pipeline was badly corroded—led not only to the shutdown of much of Prudhoe Bay and the loss of millions of dollars but also to a PR disaster that, in a single blow, undid the green reputation CEO John Browne had meticulously crafted for BP over the past decade."

—Nelson D. Schwartz, *Fortune*, October 16, 2006[2]

"When you are in the penalty box a lot, the referee is always looking for you. A pin drop becomes a bomb drop. We have to live like that."

—Ed Zander, CEO, Motorola[3]

On March 23, 2005, at 1:20 p.m., a fiery explosion occurred in Texas City, Texas, at oil major BP's largest American refinery. Fifteen people died and 170 were injured. The Texas City disaster was one of the worst industrial accidents in U.S. history.

Within hours of the explosion, BP's then–Group Chief Executive Lord John Browne arrived at the scene. "I've been with BP for a very long time now, for 38 years, and it is the worst tragedy that I've known during my time with the company," the chief executive told the press.[4] Browne toured the explosion area and spoke to refinery management, operators, technicians, and emergency responders.

BP promptly constructed a web site (www.bpresponse.org) where employees and the public could access information about the tragic explosion. The site contained news updates, inquiry contact information, government and regulatory links, on-scene coordinator contact information, press releases, and mailing list options. The site encouraged questions and answers. Its home page provided telephone numbers for worried families to call, employee assistance program contacts, and information for those seeking property-claim information. BP regularly updated the site as news unfolded.

In May 2005, BP issued an interim report that attributed the explosion to employees' failure to follow safety procedures. It amounted to "pointing fingers":

> If ISOM [isomerization] unit managers had properly supervised the start-up or if ISOM unit operators had followed procedures or taken corrective action earlier, the explosion would not have occurred. . . . The failure of ISOM unit managers to provide appropriate leadership and the failure of hourly workers to follow written procedures are among the root causes of this incident.[5]

The statement angered union leaders, employees, and victims' families, who accused BP of unfairly shifting responsibility for safety lapses to lower-level employees. The *Houston Chronicle* took the company to task.

BP apologized and asserted that poor word choice may have erroneously implied blame when there had been no intent to point fingers at anyone. BP spokesperson Hugh Depland expressed regret. "We simply used the wrong language to describe the report's findings," he explained. BP meant that they had only isolated the precursors leading to the blast, not necessarily the blast's "root cause." To leave no doubt where responsibility lay, Depland unequivocally concluded: "Our fault."[6]

In late June 2005, the U.S. Chemical Safety and Hazard Investigation Board's lead investigator Don Holmstrom reported that ". . . several key pieces of process instrumentation malfunctioned on the day of the accident. Alarms that should have warned operators of abnormal conditions in the isomerization unit did not go off."[7] Holmstrom cited BP's full cooperation as having been integral to the investigation.

Three months after the explosion, BP Products North America announced a new office opening in Texas City to house 400 BP employees.[8] Texas City's mayor applauded BP's selection and loyalty to the city. Several months later, BP agreed to pay a record U.S. safety fine of $21 million and arranged with the U.S. Occupational Safety and Health Administration (OSHA) to take corrective actions at the refinery. BP promised to hire a process expert to review refinery safety and assign an organizational expert to examine internal communications. It also agreed to upgrade its health and safety training. The oil major hinted that it expected to invest over $1 billion at the refinery over the next five years for refinery maintenance and improvements.

BP indicated that it did not intend to ignore the need for change. As Lord John Browne stated: "There has been a monumental shift for the company, and for me personally. I am 58 but can still learn, and we need to go back and ask ourselves what we are doing and what we should do differently now."[9]

Although there would be further problems for BP one year later—its Alaskan pipelines at Prudhoe Bay corroded, leading to a massive oil spill—BP never hesitated in its attempt to learn from the Texas City disaster and take the heat. Even as litigation inevitably mounted in the months following the explosion, BP continued to funnel millions of dollars into perfecting its safety rules, establishing an advisory group, hiring a retired U.S. federal justice as ombudsman, and placing $1.6 billion aside for refinery victims. A decade-long "root-and-branch" review was set in motion to overhaul all global BP practices and operations.

The oil giant brought in new CEOs to run BP North America and the Alaskan unit. New BP North American CEO Robert Malone reaffirmed the importance of improving safety and internal communications: "What you can expect from me is that I will focus on rebuilding the safety and integrity of BP's U.S. operations. With that, our reputation will move with what we do, not what we say."[10]

At the request of federal investigators, BP initiated an independent safety review panel led by well-respected former U.S. Secretary of State Howard Baker to report on the explosion. On January 17, 2007, the panel released its findings indicating that BP and its top management " . . . did not always ensure that adequate resources were effectively allocated to support or sustain a high level of safety in the industrial process and rotated refinery chiefs too quickly."[11]

Browne said that he took responsibility for the company's oversights: "BP gets it. And I get it too. This happened on my watch, and as chief executive, I have a responsibility to learn from what has occurred."[12] Browne further declared that the company had already begun to apply changes and would implement all of the panel's recommendations. At a news conference several days earlier, Lord Browne announced that he was cutting short his expected term of office by 17 months.

The Texas City explosion was a reputation catastrophe for BP. People had died and been injured. BP was continually in the headlines. BP's own internal investigation unsympathetically identified senior managers who neglected their responsibilities at the refinery. Compounding its errors, the U.S. Chemical Safety and Hazard Investigation Board's preliminary findings revealed that internal BP documents, dating back years before the blast, revealed knowledge of major safety problems at the Texas City refinery.

The findings of the Baker Panel only confirmed and expanded on these disturbing findings. Yet, despite the pounding to its reputation and the errors in judgment that resulted in its interim report, BP ultimately exhibited many of the elements that make up the first four steps of the rescue stage of reputation recovery that are discussed in this chapter—taking the heat, communicating tirelessly, facing critics, and getting the house in order.

BP Group Chief Executive Lord Browne faced the refinery tragedy head on, communicated diligently, established priorities, and listened to critics. For the most part, BP's quick response and laudatory web site initially kept BP's image intact. The ensuing media refinery coverage managed to stay relatively local. The general public also seemed to assume that the incident was a one-time tragedy. In fact, many scandal-sensitive socially responsible investment funds did not downgrade BP's investment grade after the Texas Refinery disaster.[13] Browne's early words and actions did much to reassure those affected that BP's resources would be made fully available to them and conveyed the company's appreciation for everyone's support.

By appointing a new North American CEO and assigning a chief investigator to root out the accident's causes, Browne bolstered his credibility. Browne's humble and swift response set the right tone of concern, action, and seriousness. Unfortunately, his credibility quotient would change over time as more facts pointed away from a very serious, though isolated, incident to a fundamental lapse in BP's safety culture.

Browne's prompt removal of two top executives made it abundantly clear that responsibility rests with the company's leadership and that this horrific incident reached the very top of the organization. As a Texas City refinery employee told a *Fortune* reporter: "The values are real, but they haven't been aligned with our business practices in the field. A scream at our level is, if anything, a whisper at their level."[14] BP's sincerity may not have been in question, but its behaviour and communications channels certainly were.

For years, BP had worked hard at building its image as a transparent, responsive, and environmentally friendly company. BP consistently received kudos from investors, nongovernmental organizations (NGOs), and civil society groups for its sustainability practices and precautionary stances on global climate change. Then came the Texas City explosion, Prudhoe Bay, and alleged propane price fixing in 2006. After this agonizing series of reputation blunders, BP was accused of greenwashing by friends and foes alike. The criticism was swift, scathing, and highly visible.

However, for an employee at the Texas City refinery to still have faith in the company by stating that BP's "values are real" demonstrates that

BP had built a strong foundation on which to rehabilitate its reputation. This will ease the long and painful road to recovery that lies ahead.

STEP 1: TAKE THE HEAT—LEADER FIRST

A single corporate leader, almost always the CEO, must serve as the official spokesperson during troubled times. The reputation of the CEO and company are inextricably linked.[15] CEOs are regarded by many stakeholders as the human face of the organization. However, just as CEOs receive most of the credit when things go right, they are also expected to accept the majority of the blame when things go wrong, particularly in times of crisis. Different spokespeople are advisable when the CEO or management team is implicated in an unfolding scandal or public relations disaster. Alternative representatives to the CEO might include the chairman, board member, lead director, or retired CEO.

Beyond the natural link between CEO and the company, there are advantages to having a CEO serve as the official spokesperson during a crisis. Having one person act as the single repository of communications fosters more focused, consistent, and concentrated messages. It allows the company to speak with a single voice, avoiding conflicting positions and misstatements that could confuse audiences and damage credibility at a time when trust is paramount.

To strengthen leadership credibility during crisis, CEOs must communicate transparently and proactively rather than defensively. In the early stages of corporate crisis, leaders' messages cannot be speculative or vary even slightly. Prior media training is a must for all CEOs as they assume a stronger role as the chief communicator during crises.

If a chief executive is viewed as trustworthy, it can work to a company's benefit when dealing with a crisis. During the summer of 2001, McDonald's Chairman and CEO Jack Greenberg faced a crisis that amounted to a CEO's worst nightmare. McDonald's had just learned from the FBI that two of its immensely popular promotions ("Who Wants to Be a Millionaire" and "Monopoly") had been rigged for at least six years.

Millions of Americans had participated in these games, hoping to be instant winners. McDonald's had awarded more than $10 million in top prize money to fraudulent winners because of a scam perpetrated by the marketing firm hired by the company to run the contests. The FBI had approached Greenberg for help. According to the FBI, no current or former McDonald's employees were implicated in the fraud scheme. FBI agents requested that McDonald's continue operating the rigged "Monopoly" summer promotion so that agents could gather sufficient evidence to justify a court-ordered wiretap that the FBI believed would result in capturing and convicting the culprits.

As CEO, Greenberg faced numerous agonizing and tough decisions:

- Should he launch "Monopoly" in July, aware that his customers could not possibly win, in effect knowingly defrauding them?
- Would involvement tarnish the McDonald's brand name?
- Would the inevitable drawn-out lawsuits make a bad situation even worse?
- Would employees, franchisees, the board of directors, and the media believe that he had made the right decision?
- Would they blame McDonald's for not properly managing the marketing company that McDonald's had hired and with whom McDonald's had worked with for two and a half decades?
- Would Greenberg win or lose the confidence and trust of his biggest supporters?
- Would his reputation as CEO of McDonald's be forever damaged?

Greenberg acted swiftly. He decided to cooperate with the FBI and launched the promotion on July 11, 2001. One month later, the FBI arrested one security officer and seven others from the marketing firm.

In an attempt to make things right for its customers, McDonald's immediately announced a five-day Labor Day sweepstakes featuring a $10 million prize pool. "We want you to have what belongs to you," McDonald's announced, "That includes a chance to win . . . and a chance to win big."[16] In an Open Letter to McDonald's Customers placed in newspapers across all 50 U.S. states and on television,

Greenberg stated, "This special second chance is all about making things right for you . . . and nothing is more important to us than your trust."[17]

Greenberg chose wisely and McDonald's survived the crisis seemingly unscathed. Why did this work? Greenberg's credibility was already high, he made an informed and prompt decision, and he demonstrated that he deserved the public's continued trust. Clearly, it could have gone the other way in what seemed to be a no-win situation.

Cooperating with the FBI and running an unwinnable sweepstakes might enrage customers, while not cooperating might look like McDonald's was condoning illegal acts or, even worse, covering up the company's involvement in a fraudulent scheme. What allowed McDonald's to avoid this Hobson's choice was none other than the reputation and good standing of the fast-food company and its CEO. Stakeholders had confidence in Greenberg's integrity. They believed that he would not tolerate impropriety and that he sincerely cared for his customers. The result: When the story broke, only one major paper among the slew of articles reporting on the story questioned McDonald's involvement or blamed McDonald's in any way, creating a textbook study of a CEO expertly handling a crisis.

Leaders must never underestimate the scope or depth of a burning issue or crisis. The natural tendency is to believe that the company's problem will blow over, go unnoticed, or fade away as new headlines emerge. Former Mayor Rudy Giuliani did not allow the September 11 Twin Towers' collapse to prevent him from immediately taking charge on that fatal day despite scant information and massive confusion. In contrast, the U.S. government's delayed response to Hurricane Katrina underscored what happens when leaders fail to take events at face value and act quickly.

For a CEO to lead effectively during times of crisis is an essential component of early reputation rescue. By acting promptly with one voice, transparently, and decisively, CEOs can stabilize an unstable situation and set the right tone that, in many cases, ultimately defines the crisis.

Face Head On

Part of what it means to lead in times of crisis is to avoid equivocation. Not all CEOs can be expected to be Churchills. However, when facing a crisis, CEOs should act with a statesman-like degree of firmness and confidence in their statements and solutions. Of course, there are times when a position must be adjusted if it is later found to be inconsistent with the company's values or unfolding facts.

BP backtracked from its earlier statement that seemed to shift blame for the Texas City refinery disaster from upper to lower management. BP's wavering over who was at fault cost it some reputational equity at the time. However, in retrospect, it avoided further showdowns as investigators later revealed that senior management played a larger role in overlooking early warning signs than they first thought. Although changing company position may be wise under such circumstances, public consensus building or testing the waters is to be avoided during moments of crisis.

Whether a political leader or corporate chieftain, taking a leadership stand in the early stages of an emergency is what counts. "There will be no amnesty," declared President Ronald Reagan in 1981. His uncompromising words were intended for federal air traffic controllers who threatened a nationwide airplane strike on August 3, 1981, in direct violation of governmental rules prohibiting strikes by public employees.

The controllers went on strike, nevertheless, grounding more than half of the nation's 14,000 daily flights.[18] New York City airports were inoperable, and daily losses were estimated at over $100 million.[19] Two airliners nearly collided after taking off from LaGuardia Airport. President Reagan did not argue with the right of workers in the private sector to strike but took a firm stand when it came to the government sector: "If they do not report for work within 48 hours they have forfeited their jobs and will be terminated. The law is very explicit. They are breaking the law."[20] Although the labor union took offense with the president's actions, the majority of the public supported his decision. In fact, 64 percent of Americans approved of Reagan's response to the air traffic controllers' strike.[21]

The president moved swiftly. He terminated 12,000 air traffic controllers and banned them from ever working for the Federal Aviation Administration (FAA). Reagan did not waver, seek consensus, or procrastinate on an issue that was non-negotiable. Reagan's decisiveness kept the controllers' strike from spinning out of control, while maintaining his credibility at a difficult time. The president's reputation and that of his administration were enhanced.

Just as presidents and CEOs are required to act decisively and quickly when trouble arrives, boards must, too. As difficult as it was for aerospace leader Boeing to dismiss CEO Harry Stonecipher in March 2005 for having improper relations with a senior company executive, the board acted promptly and resolutely. Boeing was already scandal-ridden when Stonecipher was brought back from retirement to replace longtime CEO Phil Condit, who presided over a reputation-damaging Pentagon procurement scandal. Stonecipher's mandate from the board was to restore the aerospace giant's sullied ethical reputation.

It was this directive to reestablish company propriety at Boeing that forced the board to confront the facts about married Stonecipher's misbehavior. After all, Stonecipher required that each Boeing employee sign a newly drafted code of conduct after his arrival. Stonecipher failed to practice what he had so solemnly preached.

When the board first learned about Stonecipher's affair, they wisely recognized that the CEO had shown poor judgment and had to be treated as any other employee. The board sought no excuses for the CEO, whom they had hoped would bring Boeing out from the shadows of scandal. The board was starkly candid about why Stonecipher had to resign, and never flinched from explaining that ethical code violations would not be tolerated. Boeing's board set an example of responsible and unfaltering corporate governance during a catastrophic ethical breach. Boeing is further discussed in Chapter 6.

RadioShack's early indecisiveness about its CEO's misleading resume contrasts with Boeing board's unwavering resolution. RadioShack's board learned from a 2006 *Fort Worth Star-Telegram* report that their CEO, Dave Edmondson, may not have told the whole truth about his educational background. At first, the board stood behind Edmondson, stating that they were hiring a law firm to investigate the situation. However, soon after the incident began making daily headlines and more facts were uncovered, the board reversed course and asked for the CEO's resignation. The unfortunate incident was having a negative effect on the CEO's credibility and the board's judgment. Although events such as these unfold swiftly, boards must not waver too long and must communicate as if the company's entire reputation were on the line—because it is.

Despite an overwhelming desire for companies and leaders to find a way to maintain the status quo, they must face the often brutal facts and confront reality. Taking the heat, communicating clearly and unequivocally, and accepting any negative consequences resulting from corporate wrongdoing are the first steps leaders can take toward rescuing a company's reputation from further erosion.

Share the Pain

Perhaps the best way for accepting responsibility and demonstrating empathy for those affected in a crisis is the apology. For the most part, apologies have been extremely effective. In fact, research has found that higher share prices generally follow corporate apologies within one year.[22] The apology is one way to help shift the focus from what has happened to what should happen next. Apologies can sometimes serve as the second bookend to a crisis, and shorten its longevity and lessen its sting. For this reason, the straightforward CEO apology has become an increasingly common strategy for dealing with a breaking crisis or its immediate aftermath.

The number of CEO and other public figure mea culpas has soared—from media celebrity Oprah Winfrey's apology for defending James Frey's book to former Harvard President Larry Summers's misgivings over his negative comments about women in science and engineering. Another example came from News Corporation Chairman Rupert Murdoch, who apologized for causing pain to the families of Ron Goldman and Nicole Brown-Simpson for planning to publish O. J. Simpson's *If I Did It* book on his wife's brutal murder. Leadership apologies have now crossed regional lines. Korean CEOs sometimes apologize in hopes of reducing fines, as do Japanese CEOs when their companies do not make earnings. Corporate regrets are fast becoming a global phenomenon.

Henry Paulson Jr., former chairman and CEO of Goldman Sachs Group, demonstrated how a properly issued and frank apology from the top can help repair a personal and company reputation. During a question-and-answer session at a Salomon Smith Barney conference in January 2003, Paulson seemed to imply that between 80 and 85 percent of Goldman Sachs's employees were irrelevant to the company's success. "I don't want to sound heartless," the CEO said, "but in almost every one of our businesses, there are 15 to 20 percent of the people who really add 80 percent of the value. I think we can cut a fair amount and not get into muscle and still be very well-positioned for the upturn."[23]

Paulson's comments drew an immediate and overwhelmingly negative reaction. Rather than wallow in explanations as to what he actually intended to say, or suggest that the comment was taken out of context, Paulson took the heat. He did not waver. In a voice mail message afterwards to all 20,000 Goldman Sachs Group employees, Paulson acknowledged that his remarks were "insensitive" and "glib." He apologized. He articulated exactly what made his comments offensive and contradictory to the financial services firm's team-oriented mind-set: ". . . the eighty-twenty rule is totally at odds with the way I think about the people here."[24] In his voice mail remarks, he commented that he intended to apologize in person at a series of upcoming town hall meetings, but realized that he should not wait. He reaffirmed the importance of teamwork over individual glory and acknowledged that he was embarrassed by his choice of words.

Paulson's apology was not a sign of weakness, but an act of strength. Within Paulson's apology are several lessons:

- *First, take responsibility.* Paulson acknowledged the distastefulness of his remarks, took full responsibility for having made them, and expressed regret.
- *Second, act quickly.* Paulson issued his voice mail apology to employees a few days after making his ill-conceived remarks.

- *Third, communicate sincerity.* Paulson accomplished this by selecting the correct channels to express his apology. Voice mail and town hall meetings allowed his genuineness to resonate with employees. An e-mail could have easily been misinterpreted and, without the sound of his voice, undoubtedly have carried far less emotional weight.

The difference between an effective and ineffective apology can be startling. Consider the markedly different ways that CEOs at Fortune 500 companies Citigroup and Sony handled crises that required apologies from the top. Citigroup's Chief Executive Charles "Chuck" Prince apologized for problems that eventually led to the collapse of its Japanese private banking license. Prince bowed deeply and symbolically for a long seven seconds at a Tokyo news conference (as seen in Exhibit 4.1). The global media widely captured his bent image, which powerfully communicated Prince's recognition that he was accountable and that silence was unacceptable. He also sent the symbolic signal that he respected Japanese customs and bowed in regret.

Carol Ballock, CEO campaign strategist and consultant for the most sought-after speaking podiums, refers to Prince's apology as "the seven-second bow heard around the world."[25] Soon after, Prince promptly fired three high-ranking executives connected to the scandal and closed another Tokyo banking unit to investigate any further violations. Without delay, the CEO launched a company-wide "shared responsibility" program to instill employee values deep within the organization. By taking these actions, Prince quickly and sincerely took full responsibility for the problem and initiated sound steps to prevent any reoccurrence.

In contrast, the apology by Howard Stringer, CEO of electronics innovator Sony, for the widespread overheating of Sony's lithium-ion batteries that sometimes burst laptops into flames appeared half-hearted. At first, Sony erroneously stated that the problems lay with its customers' laptops and not the batteries. Even though media and online coverage became increasingly widespread with dramatic videos of fiery laptops and computer recalls blaming Sony batteries, Sony executives made no

Citigroup apologises to Japan

Chief executives' public bow of remorse for illegal actions at private banking unit aims to rebuild public trust

By David Ibison in Tokyo

Citigroup apologised publicly yesterday for the worst breakdown of corporate behaviour in more than 100 years of doing business in Japan and announced plans to win back public and regulatory trust.

The US bank, the world's largest, has been punished by the Financial Services Agency, the banking regulator, for a series of serious breaches and was ordered on September 17 to close its private banking operation in Japan.

Yesterday it said it would also close its investment management and real estate advisory units there.

Charles Prince, Citigroup chief executive, said: "I sincerely apologise to customers and the public for the company's failure to comply with legal and regulatory requirements in Japan."

He admitted senior staff in the private bank had put "short-term profits ahead of the bank's long-term reputation" and broken the law – "a unique breakdown in Japan due to the individuals involved".

An FSA investigation showed failure of Citigroup Japan's internal control and lack of oversight from the US led to transgressions that permitted "large profits" to be "amassed illegally".

The breaches had led to the US corporation doing business with "anti-social elements" – organised crime and money launderers – and when quizzed by FSA inspectors, some managers "pro-

vided responses that differed from the truth," the FSA said.

The FSA also found Citigroup had failed to correct problems revealed in 2001 but had told the regulator it had done so.

In a miserable year for the bank which has seen it settle a $2.5bn lawsuit, put aside $5.2bn to cover other legal actions and apologise for disrupting the electronic European bond market, Mr Prince flew to Japan to apologise

in person to Hirofumi Gomi, FSA commissioner, and bowed in public to appeal to the Japanese taste for public displays of remorse.

The bank yesterday announced upgraded compliance systems, including new management, new reporting lines for management and more independent compliance.

The problems in Japan have already claimed the scalps of three of the bank's most senior

executives: Sir Deryck Maughan, chairman of Citigroup International; Thomas Jones, head of investment management; and Peter Scaturro, head of its private bank. In Japan, 12 executives have left the company, 11 had wage cuts and others have been reprimanded.

In New York yesterday the National Association of Securities Dealers fined Citigroup $250,000 for "inappropriate" sales

literature. Citigroup neither admitted nor denied the allegations.

■ Carrefour has dropped the bank as financial adviser on the sale of the French retailer's Japan operations because of concerns over the bank's reputation.

Additional reporting by David Wells in New York and Lina Saigol in London

French disconnection, Page 20

Mea culpa: Charles Prince (right), Citigroup chief executive, and Douglas Peterson, Citibank Japan CEO, bow in apology during a news conference in Tokyo AFP

EXHIBIT **4.1**   *Deep Apology*

Source: *Financial Times*, October 25, 2004.

public comments. Only several months later did Sony announce a massive global recall of 9.6 million lithium-ion batteries.

Instead of CEO Stringer's apologizing for the lithium battery manufacturing production problem, Sony corporate Executive Officer Yutaka Nakagawa offered the apology. Rather than a full bow at the press conference, the electronics division executive bowed less deeply and from a sitting position. This action signaled that the problems were not considered by Sony's top management as all that serious. The apology was noted but only partially halted negative media coverage of the problem.

Sony's product-quality problems continue to haunt its reputation, raising doubts about Stringer's ability to turn around this once-unstoppable company. The battery debacle is frequently mentioned in media coverage as one of the year's biggest public relations disasters. As one equity analyst commented in Tokyo, the battery problem was "definitely making a dent in Sony's image."[26] To be fair, Stringer remarked in an interview post–battery crisis that he spent too much time deferring to his Japanese colleagues about avoiding public comments. However, the remark gave the impression to some that he was not taking responsibility for the problem.[27] Stringer said that he intends to start taking his own counsel.

It is not easy for a CEO to apologize and declare fault. In part, the reason may simply be human reluctance to admit error. Barbara Kellerman, research director of the Center for Public Leadership at Harvard's John F. Kennedy School of Government, suggests that there are many other reasons for executive reluctance. A CEO, for example, may simply not believe that the company did anything wrong or does not want to upset internal factions. Executives may be concerned about their legacy or do not want to lose competitive advantage. Or reluctance to apologize, as discussed more fully later in this chapter, may simply mean that a CEO is heeding legal advice.[28]

Because CEO apologies have become too commonplace, what were once highly effective means to regain reputation and halt further damage are losing their effectiveness. In Weber Shandwick's *Safeguarding Reputation*™ study, global business executives reported that other strategies such as outlining next steps worked better in helping companies recover reputation post-crisis than apologies. Out of a list of 14 possible reputation recovery steps, CEO apologies ranked eighth, as seen in Exhibit 4.2.

Although apologies from the top are necessary but clearly not all there is to rescuing reputation, companies and their CEOs should follow Kellerman's advice about the elements of the perfect apology. She stresses acknowledging the mistake, taking responsibility quickly, expressing regret, being timely, and providing assurance that it will not happen again.[29] In addition to Kellerman's suggestions, CEO apologies must be

EXHIBIT **4.2** *Best Ways to Start Reputation Recovery after Crisis*

	Total Global Executives	North America	Europe	Asia
Announce specific actions company will take to fix the problem	76%	83%	73%	78%
Establish early warning system	76	83	69	82
Establish specific policies and goals demonstrating corporate responsibility	73	75	69	74
Make sure legal team approves all statements	72	74	68	76
Issue regular public progress reports addressing the problem	71	78	69	70
Disclose quickly and publicly what happened	71	73	72	70
Determine if problem is industry-wide or limited to the company before acting	67	60	68	62
Provide public apology from CEO or Chairman	59	57	57	64
Achieve quarterly earnings goals	57	50	59	47
Create senior position with specific responsibility for managing company reputation	47	45	50	42
Avoid any public communications until all facts are in	45	46	39	46
Respond to bloggers who have facts wrong	39	31	40	41
Restructure or eliminate board members	26	14	27	21
Keep the CEO out of the media	20	16	21	17

Note: Results for Brazilian executives are included in the total.
Source: Weber Shandwick *Safeguarding Reputation*™ with KRC Research, 2006.

followed up with action. Otherwise, these mea culpas will appear as mere window dressing, and stakeholders will continue to doubt the company's credibility and ability to recover.

STEP 2: COMMUNICATE TIRELESSLY

Communicating effectively and often during a crisis is essential. As General Motors CEO Rick Waggoner explained as he worked to turn around the world's largest automotive manufacturer: "People are always hungrier for information when times are challenging."[30] Crises create unsettling ambiguities. Companies facing crisis are usually under siege from the media, the financial community, disgruntled employees, online and offline critics, and in some cases, their boards. Rescuing reputation and taking the first steps on the path to long-term recovery require a greater level of communications than is typical in less stressful times. Communications from the top are needed in heavy doses to steady employees who may be reeling from bad news and uncertainty. It is a leader's job to choose the most effective channels and the right words, and then give communications their most meaning during challenging times.

Speaking at Stanford graduate school, Xerox turnaround CEO Anne Mulcahy essentially concurred with Waggoner on the importance of strong communications during crisis. Faced with turning around the once languishing Xerox as described earlier in Chapter 3, Mulcahy noted that "I feel like my title should be Chief Communication Officer, because that's really what I do. When I became CEO, I spent the first 90 days on planes traveling to various offices and listening to anyone who had a perspective on what was wrong with the company. I think if you spend as much time listening as talking, that's time well spent."[31] Like Waggoner's advice, Mulcahy's counsel is sound. In a business climate where every employee, customer, and shareholder has equal access to bad news, two-way CEO communications are essential for recovery.

In the aftermath of Hurricane Katrina, the New Orleans utility and nuclear company Entergy faced a series of daunting challenges requiring

EXHIBIT **4.3** *Employee Message from Entergy CEO Wayne Leonard*

September 2, 2005

In every man and woman's life, there is a defining moment. It is a brief intersection of circumstances and choices that define a person for better or worse, a life of unfilled potential or a life that mattered, that made a difference.

It is true of individuals and it is true of business. We have great passion for the difference we make in others' lives. We provide a commodity that sustains life. But, more importantly, we provide the most precious commodity of all—hope.

Right now, many of our employees are hard pressed to be hopeful or optimistic as their homes and workplaces have been destroyed, their lives turned upside-down and their families scattered or still missing from the historical disaster that is Hurricane Katrina.

But, be assured that Entergy is a just and compassionate organization. The actions we will be taking to support our employees will reflect that.

The task before us is awesome but not insurmountable. We will be challenged at every turn but this is what has always defined Entergy. We are at our best when the challenge is greatest. But, what defines us is the moral courage, when we stand at the crossroads between light and dark, to always choose light. It is a clear-eyed focus not only on our success, but for the betterment of those around us.

Our response to this crisis will make the people we call Entergy remembered and revered for all time. It won't be simply because we rebuilt our devastated system after the greatest natural disaster in the nation's history. That is given. It will be because of the passion and compassion that drives our every waking thought and action.

I have no doubt that there is plenty of work before us before we even approach a place called "normal." I also have no doubt in the talent and dedication and spirit of you, the people that are Entergy.

We are bruised but not broken. We are saddened but not despondent. We are at that remarkable place in time where hearts, minds and souls of the good cross with challenge and opportunity to set the course of history. We define ourselves here and now for all to see, everywhere.

God bless you and please stay safe.

J. Wayne Leonard

extensive internal and external communications. Nearly 2,000 employees were evacuated and lost homes and possessions, and were separated from family and friends. Corporate headquarters was forced to relocate temporarily to Clinton, Mississippi. CEO Wayne Leonard e-mailed letters to all 14,000 employees regularly, used their online newsletter *Inside Entergy*, and launched StormNet, a special web site for employees and their families.

Leonard's first daily e-mail message (see Exhibit 4.3) arrived just a few days after Hurricane Katrina hit and reflects the honest, hopeful, and heartfelt words of a CEO at a defining moment in his company's history. The CEO e-mails were also printed in a daily newsletter delivered to major worksites for the line crews who did not have e-mail access. Leonard's compassionate words went far in reassuring employees that he was an engaged, concerned leader, and was going to be reaching out to them on a regular basis.

No stone was left unturned at Entergy in communicating with stakeholders during this catastrophic event. In the absence of much of the local media that had evacuated New Orleans, much like many of Entergy's employees, Entergy increased its efforts to communicate information to the public and engaged a largely national press corps to correct any misperceptions about local conditions. Communications to all audiences was part of its rescue plan. Necessity was the mother of invention and Entergy's reputation and recovery was better for it.[32]

Communications during difficult times must combine regular and timely face-to-face contact, electronic exchanges, and hard-copy messaging. At Entergy, CEO Leonard and the senior management team visited field operations and were present at the command center and communicated across media channels that best reached all target audiences. Unfortunately, too many leaders rely too heavily on electronic communications to relay news about unfolding problems.

Personal meetings in small or large groups can do more for rallying the troops in rebuilding a company's reputation than sanitized and consensus-driven messaging. Personal connections are hard to replicate on paper and online. In this early phase of reputation recovery, personal connections promote a feeling of a shared purpose, and keep employees working productively and with the company's interests in mind. Without a personal connection, companies find it harder to recover. Employees in crisis-ridden companies are often open to entreaties by competitors and can become as cynical as the company's fiercest critics.

The need for personal contact notwithstanding, companies still need to pay rapt attention to their online web site communications. Even in more stable times, the Internet is so integral to modern living that the quantity and quality of information on a company web site has a lasting effect on a company's reputation. In times of emergency varying from natural disaster, product recalls, and executive turnover to disturbing rumors and troublesome world events, the company web site is likely to be the first place many stakeholders—customers, media, and employees—go for information. The web site's effect on reputation during these trying times becomes exponentially greater. Stakeholders place high value on immediacy and accuracy. Companies under scrutiny must be responsive and communicate continuously.

The September 11 terrorist attacks had a profound impact on how companies communicate online. For the first time, many sites became a critical crisis-management tool, eclipsing other forms of traditional communications. Within hours, web sites that were once devoted almost exclusively to industry information and general business news were inundated with tragedy-related inquiries from employees and Internet surfers who would not have otherwise visited. Many companies responded by incorporating into their sites the latest news reports, sympathy messages, and information on how to volunteer and make donations.

Although most companies responded to the national crisis in some way within the first week after September 11, most sites did not provide e-mail addresses of people to contact for further information. Many companies missed an important opportunity to build their reputations as leaders in calming employees, customers, shareholders, and other stakeholders. BP's web site after the Texas City refinery explosion is a good example of responding quickly and continuously. Today, online crisis communication is a best practice for most companies around the world.

Tireless communications are needed in every phase of reputation recovery. In the earliest stages, communications must be on all the time.

Disclose Honestly and Quickly

Brutal honesty is not easy when facing up to bad news. Yet that is what Brazilian-born Carlos Ghosn did when, after rising through the ranks at Renault and Michelin, he arrived in Japan in 1999 with a mandate to revive Nissan, the then–rapidly deteriorating global automotive company. Renault CEO Louis Schweitzer dispatched Ghosn with instructions to stop the bleeding, perhaps one of the toughest challenges in corporate history. After three short months, Ghosn unveiled his Nissan Revival Plan (NRP) to a worldwide media and trade press. His candor was astonishing. Ghosn focused on three numbers:

1. Nissan had dropped from a 6.6 percent to 4.9 percent worldwide market share since 1991.
2. Nissan's annual vehicle production had fallen by 600,000.
3. Nissan had been unprofitable since 1991, nearly a decade, and was now anticipating a loss of over $6 billion.

Ghosn, the new CEO, straightforwardly laid out Nissan's goals for revival. He would reduce suppliers, close factories, cut jobs, streamline purchasing, and trim general expenses. Ghosn publicly announced the steps needed for Nissan's success and the standards by which its success would be measured.

The advantage of such transparency, especially where the disclosed facts are so negative, is that it gets all the bad news out at once. Frank and candid communications such as Ghosn's helped to establish a baseline from which they could begin measuring progress toward recovery. When bad news is released little by little, the crisis at hand is simply prolonged, the rescue process stalls, and reestablishing stakeholder confidence is postponed. Even when continuing problems are anticipated, credibility can be maintained if all disclosures are accurate and future problems are candidly acknowledged.

For this reason Grant Thornton Chief Executive David McDonnell did his very best to admit that the international reputation of his company was in peril and that the immediate future looked bleak. In 2004, the Italian police arrested the president and partner of the Italian branch of Grant Thornton, Parmalat's auditing firm. The police accused Grant Thornton executives of falsely certifying Parmalat's balance sheets and recommending ways for the company to defraud shareholders.[33] Preliminary investigations showed that Parmalat's books were unable to account for approximately $8.5 to $12 billion. Parmalat was fast turning into Europe's Enron.

Soon after the arrest of the Grant Thornton employees, however, McDonnell publicly acknowledged that Grant Thornton's reputation had been damaged. In a strongly worded press release on January 8, 2004, Grant Thornton stated that it had expelled its Italian affiliate, Grant Thornton SpA, from its international network. CEO McDonnell is quoted as saying: "Our first responsibility is to our clients around the world. They need to be assured of our commitment to maintain the reputation and integrity of Grant Thornton International."[34]

Candidly noting that the company would face additional troubles in the near future, he then went on: "As a result of our ongoing investigation it is clear that Grant Thornton SpA will not be able to operate in the for[e]seeable future in an effective way to protect the reputation of the Grant Thornton International name and the reputation of the other independent firms in the Grant Thornton International network."[35]

Faced with an obvious scandal, McDonnell frankly discussed the facts, took decisive action by severing ties with the Italian office, and then openly confessed that it would take time before the news got better. McDonnell had taken a deep breath, steeled himself, and communicated honestly—to his credit and the credit of his firm.

In all fairness, the hours following crises or disasters are fraught with rumors and confusion. Leaders must put aside all personal and political considerations and do what is right for the organization. If only incomplete information is known as events unfold, it is simply better to communicate that there are conflicting reports, lack of detail, or an insufficient amount of information, rather than providing eager stake-holders with information that subsequently turns out to be erroneous or disingenuous.

When taking charge during times of crisis, leaders should understand the importance of recognizing what they do not know. It is too easy to get blinded by assumptions drawn from what they do know. American Red Cross Communications Director Charles Connor recalled how pro-foundly limiting information can be during a crisis, especially during its first stages. From past experience as the U.S. Navy's public affairs director, Connor described what happened when two missiles were accidentally fired into Turkey during a routine training exercise: "When you're at headquarters and it's the first hours of the crisis . . . experience tells you that half of the information is wrong, but you don't know which half. You can only offer information you're absolutely sure is true."[36] During those first dark hours after crisis hits, leaders struggle to get a handle on what happened, but should be prepared to admit that they can only disclose what they know absolutely to be true.

The problems that befall a corporation that speculates on preconceptions, or speaks or acts out of self-interest, are legion. Perhaps one of the more serious of these situations occurred following the tragic March 11, 2004, train bombings in Madrid that killed 191 people and left more than 1,500 injured. Almost immediately, the Spanish Prime Minister Jose Aznar and other government officials blamed the Basque separatist group ETA for the attacks. Even though ETA spokespeople denied responsi-bility and information was emerging that Al Qaeda–related terrorists were responsible, the Spanish government held to its explanation. Not only did Aznar's government continue persuading the media that ETA was the culprit, but they also relayed this misinformation to the United Nations Security Council.[37]

Why the prime minister remained steadfast in his belief about ETA's culpability is unclear. Perhaps he was unwilling to accept the fact that involvement of Spanish troops in Iraq might have led to such horrifying consequences. Perhaps he simply hoped that the truth would not adversely affect the scheduled elections only days away. As the Spanish government was continuing to blame the separatist group, Islamic militants claimed responsibility. Shortly afterwards, police found bomb detonators and an Arabic audiotape reciting verses from the Koran in a nearby van. A few days later on the regularly scheduled election date, Aznar's party was voted out. The prime minister was severely criticized for mishandling information about the attack, and his party's prospects made a 180-degree turn in a matter of days.

Nor did the ill will generated by this incident quickly fade away. One year after the bombing, an investigatory special commission harshly criticized the Aznar government for not taking into account the seriousness of the Islamic militants' threats and for misleading the public. According to lawmakers, "It can be said that the government's conduct was driven exclusively . . . by party interests."[38] This conclusion underscored public sentiment that Aznar had accused the ETA of the bombings only to keep his political party in office.

The new ruling party accused the former prime minister of making Spain a prime terrorist target by deploying troops to Iraq. Aznar's political ambition cost him the election and permanently tarnished his legacy. His inability to hear the truth that the ETA was not involved in the attack, even when the evidence was directly in front of him, not only added to the tragedy's confusion but also delayed in protecting his people.

There are times when circumstances require that full disclosure is not advisable. Strict compliance with legal counsel and organizational policies has to be seriously considered when communicating during a crisis. What is important when deciding how to act and what to say is the recognition that companies are judged not only in a court of law but in the court of public opinion. In an unending climate of accounting scandals, options backdating, and government investigations, companies and their leaders may conclude that the legal risks of full disclosure are outweighed by the negative consequences of appearing vague or standing mute. Whether corporate leaders like it or not, there is a price to be paid for such a determination. In the court of public opinion, to remain silent implies guilt—rightly or wrongly.

The world's largest global employment company, Adecco SA, suffered reputation loss in January 2004 by not satisfactorily disclosing information about lax internal controls that delayed its 2003 financial filings. Adecco lost nearly one-third of its value that day as investors panicked, thinking that another Parmalat and Enron were about to emerge. The firm only released a succinct statement saying that legal constraints prevented it from elaborating on the severity of its lax internal controls.

During a conference call with investors and media a few days later, Adecco Chairman John Bowmer answered questions "with a lawyer at his side."[39] Enraged investors quickly lost confidence when Bowmer was unable to answer questions about future earnings. As one shareholder said: "As soon as it became clear the company wouldn't say anything more than was in the press release, people were disappointed and sold the stock."[40]

When CEOs have lawyers at their sides monitoring their every word, the public infers that they are not acting transparently. The Adecco chairman gave the impression that the company surely had something to hide and the worst was yet to come. He was ousted six months later. Of course, there must be a careful balance between the CEO's need to be forthcoming and the need to defer to counsel on matters that require specific legal expertise.

Reassure: Keep an Eye on Your Team

When companies find themselves on the brink of disaster, there are many unexpected dark moments. To take that first step toward a brighter future, leaders should temporarily reduce expectations and reassure those affected. For employees who are not in the decision-making or news-update loop, the early moments of crisis are frightening and overwhelming. It is only natural that employees would be concerned about job security. Will their company survive? Will their jobs still be needed? Should they not take any chances and start looking for new employment immediately?

Adding to this brew of uncertainty are the inevitable efforts by recruiters who dangle new opportunities before middle and upper management talent working at crisis-ridden companies. When .*Xerox* found its problems on the *Wall Street Journal's* front page, employees felt "wounded," according to its Director of Business Ethics and Compliance David Friskkorn.[41] To employees, a crisis is both a personal and professional matter. It jeopardizes their ability to pay their bills and manage and build their careers. Unfortunately, crises often begin unfolding with little hope of closure in the short-term.

In the face of such uncertainty, all remaining employees, management and nonmanagement alike, need reassurance and reasons to stay at the company. When McKesson merger partner HBOC lost $9 billion of its market capitalization in a single day following the disclosure of accounting fraud, CEO John Hammergren knew that employees would be devastated. Hammergren also knew that winning the hearts and minds of employees was his first priority: "I spent the first few weeks on the road seeing as many of our employees as I could. I went out and tried to calm people down."[42] Reassuring employees and showing concern is critical to rescuing a company from spiraling further downward.

In addition to the veil of uncertainty that inevitably falls over a crisis-ridden company, the initial days and months involve other work-related stresses that should not be overlooked. For some, there is a sharp workload increase as the company struggles to deal with a crisis as well as run its business. Every employee must focus their efforts on getting back to normal if the company is to surmount its problems in a reasonably timely fashion. The work environment following a crisis is almost always intense and at times debilitating.

In a December 2004 teleconference organized by the Arthur Page Society, former Merck Vice President of Public Affairs, Joan Wainwright, recounted her lessons learned from managing Merck's 2004 recall of its popular arthritis drug Vioxx. The teleconference took place a few months after the initial announcement. She wisely underscored the importance of paying close attention to the team during the immediate aftermath of a crisis.

Less than one week before the recall announcement, Wainwright pulled her public affairs team off their day jobs to help prepare 65 notification documents, logistics, audience grids, recall-ready web sites, advertising, and set up toll-free numbers. They were also asked to brainstorm two scenario outcomes and prepare contingency planning if the recall was leaked to the media earlier than planned. The public affairs team was on high alert, working closely with Merck's investor relations, legal, and marketing groups. To prepare properly and in little time, some team members had no choice but to sleep in the office and work around the clock.

While some public affairs members thrived, others folded under the pressure. As head of public affairs, Wainwright remarked that several team members whom she least expected to have difficulty dealing with the 24-hour high-stakes schedule struggled over the first few weeks. To prevent burnout, several members of the team were given a one-week break. Wainwright imposed a separation of function. She reassigned several members to a dedicated Vioxx crisis team, with a 12-month limit, and allowed others to return to their original public affairs jobs. To further firm up the crisis team, she retained several outside public relations professionals for at least 12 months. The solution to dividing up crisis and day-to-day management of the company runs parallel to the actions of Xerox's CEO Anne Mulcahy. Like Wainwright, she divided Xerox into groups, with one small group working on crisis issues while the larger group worked on daily matters, thereby effectively "fencing off"[43] the two groups.

Outside professionals are resources that many companies, not just Merck, turn to in moments of crisis. When Ed Breen walked into Tyco as the new CEO in July 2002, he had his work cut out for him. Prior CEO Dennis Kozlowski had nearly destroyed the company by illegally using company funds and tarnishing its once admirable reputation. Breen had no choice but to clean house at the highest levels. At the same time, he had to keep Tyco functioning and out of bankruptcy court. The new CEO hired outside professionals and firms to support some of Tyco's key corporate functions such as finance, legal, public relations, and human resources. The added support at the top gave Breen critical time to focus on the turnaround and on traumatized middle managers who had lost their bosses, including many of their direct reports.

Bringing in outsiders has the additional advantage of infusing the organization with new individuals who have not been tainted by the emotional baggage influencing those living through the daily grind of corporate downfalls. They also introduce new thinking and energy, creative approaches, and unconventional strategies that can overcome the stagnation often afflicting companies in crisis. Sandra Alstadt, Entergy's director of utility communications, soon realized this lesson when she brought in several outside North Eastern Entergy colleagues to help the team at command central with the aftermath of Hurricane Katrina.

At first, Alstadt thought that these Entergy "storm outsiders" would serve as extra arms and legs to help with overflowing communications activities. However, she soon learned that their fresh perspective, enthusiasm, and "compassion" were a blessing. "We saw them as additional help but ended up with an additional shot in the arm," remarked Alstadt.[44] Alstadt always keeps a list of people who can jump in and relieve a colleague who needs some time off.

In a similar scenario, when CEO Anders Moberg was brought in to lead Netherlands food retailer Royal Ahold after a massive accounting fraud hit the company, he hired well-known Dutch lawyer Peter Wakkie to manage Ahold's legal problems and former Philips finance director to temporarily address investor confidence.[45] Moberg agreed with Breen's postcrisis action at Tyco to hire a whole coterie of outside accountants, lawyers, public relations professionals, and executive recruiters: "I had a cadre around me of very senior, respected talent that had been through many wars in their lives. What I liked about it was nobody got rattled."[46]

Bringing in outsiders with clear heads and no agendas can relieve staff overburdened by managing crisis day in and day out. Although a crisis may not seem the right time to bring in new people or employees from other facilities, it is often the best strategy for helping a team do their best under stressful conditions. Weber Shandwick's U.S. Corporate Practice Chair, Micho Spring says that companies in crisis now expect their public relations firms to provide experts to work in-house until the company gets back on its feet. Spring adds, "An extra fire fighter makes a big difference in extinguishing the flames."[47]

STEP 3: DON'T UNDERESTIMATE YOUR CRITICS AND COMPETITORS

A company should not ignore or diminish what its critics and enemies have to say. They may be telling leaders something they do not want to hear but need to hear. Merck's former Public Affairs Vice President Joan Wainwright counsels companies not to be surprised by its well-organized and experienced critics. Within days of the Vioxx recall, plaintiff attorneys held conferences to share best practices and update information on class-action lawsuits against pharmaceutical companies.[48]

These critics include not only attorneys but also full-fledged pressure groups that are more than capable of facing off against the largest global corporations. Critics do not come and go but have staying power that can last for years. For example, PETA (People for the Ethical Treatment of Animals), founded over 25 years ago, was once considered a fringe movement. PETA is now the world's largest animal rights organization, with more than one million members and supporters. Its reach runs far and wide, and companies dismiss their complaints at their own peril. Professor Jim Bright of Indiana University School of Journalism advises against ignoring critics outright because they could be your customers. He notes that companies need to think twice before alienating both sides.[49]

Even a company as large and powerful as the $312 billion Wal-Mart has learned not to underestimate its critics. Two groups in particular—Wal-Mart Watch (www.walmartwatch.com) and Wake Up Wal-Mart (www.wakeupwalmart.com)—have made extensive inroads battling Wal-Mart's reputation and image. Their impact has been appreciable and impossible to ignore. CEO Lee Scott has commented to employees on their power: "Your company is the focus of one of the most well-organized and well-financed corporate campaigns in history. A coalition of unions and others are spending over $25 million this year to try to do damage to this company."[50]

These Wal-Mart opponents have done just that. A leaked internal Wal-Mart study reported that nearly 8 percent of the store's customers no longer shopped at Wal-Mart because of its reputation.[51] Since Wal-Mart has 127 million customers, the number of customers who are turning away is approximately 10 million. Lee Scott has taken critics' relentless attacks seriously and is turning the company upside down to meet expectations, win back fleeing customers, and attract new customers. As part of Wal-Mart's battle to rescue its reputation, Scott has organized its own grassroots group called Working Families for Wal-Mart (www.forwalmart.com).

Sometimes it pays to love thy enemies and keep them close. Juggernaut Texas power company TXU had been rebuilding its image for years. Although its profitability steadily improved after a major loss in 2002, TXU continuously angered its customers with high rates, poor customer focus, and antienvironmental policies.[52] In 2006, TXU decided to build nearly one dozen new coal-fired power plants. Chairman John Wilder announced that these plants would produce an extraordinarily high 78 million tons of carbon dioxide emissions into the air every year. This, of course, caught the attention of the Environmental Defense and Natural Resources Defense Council and its president, Fred Krupp. Krupp tried to get a meeting with TXU's chairman but to no avail.

The environmental group did what most savvy critics do now and launched an antisite, www.Stoptxu.com, to urge people to advocate against the carbon dioxide-emitting plants. Environmental Defense also initiated a lawsuit against the utility. The suit was before the courts when the unexpected happened. In February 2007, private-equity group Kohlberg Kravis Roberts & Co. (KKR) offered to buy TXU in the largest leveraged buyout to date. However, KKR knew from the outset that they had no desire to rebuild TXU's reputation and do battle with its fiercest critics. This was no way to recoup the utility's image.

KKR and Krupp decided to sit down and negotiate a settlement that would address the Environmental Defense's qualms. Krupp negotiated a deal with KKR that included the reduction of 11 coal plants to 3 in return for the environmentalists' blessing. KKR wisely settled with its critics and at the same time enhanced its own reputation as TXU's new owners. Krupp's persistence underscored the point that companies need to mind their critics if they want to prevent reputation-damaging events: "Going online, we shifted this from a local debate over generating electricity to a national debate over capping and reducing carbon emissions."[53]

A besieged company must also expect its arch competitor to pounce when it is weakening and its reputation is fading. Any misstep as a crisis unfolds provides competitors with the advantage they need to wreak havoc. This happened to enterprise software maker PeopleSoft on June 6, 2003, when Oracle launched a hostile takeover bid days after PeopleSoft agreed to a $1.7 billion deal with JD Edwards. Although Oracle's $5.1 billion hostile bid was not initially taken seriously and was unanimously rejected by PeopleSoft's board, Oracle appealed directly to PeopleSoft shareholders and customers.

PeopleSoft became distracted with Oracle's assault and began losing its customer grip. Oracle bought full-page newspaper advertisements urging shareholders to choose between taking "cash from Oracle" or an "uncertain future with current management." PeopleSoft responded to the attack with its own full-page advertisements in major newspapers urging customers to "show your support for PeopleSoft by moving ahead with your planned purchases of PeopleSoft products this month."

Over the ensuing battle between the two titans, PeopleSoft reported several poor quarters and eventually fired its CEO Craig Conway. After Oracle sweetened the deal to $6.3 billion, PeopleSoft was acquired by its rival several months later. Some say that PeopleSoft lost its balance during this risky and trying period. Oracle has now tried to do the same with rival SAP. Just as SAP reported a slowdown in its business, Oracle's CEO Larry Ellison attempted to tarnish its competitor's reputation by suing over stolen files.[54] The question remains how prepared SAP was for the onslaught of its competitors' tactics and how effective Oracle's reputation-busting tactics will be over the long term.

Critics and competitors are also flocking in greater numbers to the blogosphere, where their voices are amplified before often entirely new audiences. Responding to their criticisms postcrisis is a decision every company has to make as it rebuilds lost reputation. The majority of global business executives in Weber Shandwick's *Safeguarding Reputation*™ study agree that responding to bloggers postcrisis is not an effective way to begin the recovery process.[55] Fewer than 4 in 10 (39 percent) believe that engaging with bloggers who may have the facts wrong is a good idea.

Perhaps business decision makers around the globe believe that companies should concentrate on fixing the problem and understanding what went wrong before turning their attention to correcting online conversations. Or the time may be ripe to provide accurate information to highly influential bloggers who are not as informed as they may think.

Leaders must always be on the alert for the unexpected from competitors when their companies are pulling their reputations back from the brink.

STEP 4: RESET THE COMPANY CLOCK

Instilling a sense of urgency often requires getting the senior team to focus more on what has to happen next and less on what went wrong in the first place. Internal politics and finger pointing distracts leadership from attending to those critical moments when moving toward recovery is essential. Wallowing in regret and recriminations is simply not helpful and keeps the company from moving forward. Even if the company is not frozen in time by recent calamities, business as usual is unacceptable. The pace of getting things done has to be accelerated.

A good solution is shock therapy in the form of an overwhelmingly heavy dose of undeniable reality. One CEO, for example, summoned his senior team and displayed charts of its rapidly falling market share. To stun the team further into accepting the facts, he showed slides of competitors with quotes mocking the company. The shock value alone accelerated the team's drive to rescue the company from their downward spiral.

Perhaps one of the best practitioners of instilling action and new thinking through shock therapy is CEO Carlos Ghosn. As previously mentioned, when he arrived in Japan to resuscitate and repair Nissan, he found the global automotive manufacturer in dire straits. Nissan was in free-fall mode—a 27-year decline in domestic market share, 37 different board members, 43 dissimilar automotive models, less than five profitable lines, and no discernable vision.[56] Ghosn quickly isolated the reason for Nissan's catastrophic state—no urgency. As Ghosn aptly describes in his book *Shift: Inside Nissan's Historic Revival*, "The notion of time didn't exist. To my shock, whenever I brought up the question of a deadline, people told me a year for what should have taken a week, and three years for something that should have been done in three months. I quickly realized I was going to have to reset the company clock."[57]

The new Nissan CEO grasped that the only way to instill a sense of urgency in the organization and get people to change how they were working was to yell "Fire!"[58] The "burning platform" concept is not new in business turnarounds but still remains the fastest way to get everyone to pay attention to the rising flames engulfing a company. Reputations can be mended only when individuals realize that there has been a tear in the company's fabric that needs to be immediately repaired.

Referring to his previously discussed straightforward, eye-opening public announcement of Nissan's troubles three months after first arriving, Ghosn explained: "The shock of my announcement was part of Nissan's therapy. My task had been to make public opinion, both outside and (especially) within the company, understand and admit that Nissan had reached the point of no return."[59] Ghosn kindled a fire under Nissan's employees, both management and nonmanagement alike. Their choice was clear—either change and escape the flames of economic disaster or be consumed by it.

Adding to the solemnity of Nissan's position, the CEO ended his surprising announcement with an unexpected, yet frank, personal commitment. Ghosn said that if Nissan did not meet its goals within the designated time frame, he would resign and so would each member of his executive team![60] By painting a realistic picture of the company's perilous situation, and by tying his own career and those of his top management team to reaching Nissan's goals, Ghosn was able to communicate the dire nature of Nissan's position. He also put himself and management in the same boat as all Nissan's employees. The Nissan boat would either stay afloat through the collective effort of all or they would sink together. Ghosn publicly faced reality as an initial first step to keeping the company from slipping further under water. He was brutally honest, straightforward, and told it like it is. To get Nissan on the move once again was a matter of the deepest urgency.

Carl-Henric Svanberg is another CEO who found himself encircled by fire. As the first outsider CEO in 60 years to lead the mobile telecommunications network Ericsson, Svanberg is credited with the company's turnaround. From 2001 to 2003, Ericsson experienced falling stock prices, massive job cuts, and dwindling market share. Three years later, Ericsson was back on its feet and out of imminent danger. Svanberg explains: "When you have a crisis, the crisis itself becomes one of your biggest assets if that crisis is bad enough. Everyone gets very modest and humble and listens. If you need to do rough things, you do rough things."[61] Although turnarounds are tough enough, Svanberg let it be known to his workforce that it was all or nothing: "We had only one bullet, only one shot to make it right."[62]

There is no room for complacency or status quo in turnarounds. From the top floor to the shop floor, everyone has to help stop the bleeding. Crisis gives leaders permission to instill that sense of urgency and focus on change.

Break into Easy Pieces

Turning around corporate failure is an overwhelming task. Once the company is forced to look forward rather than backward, and a healthy sense of urgency is settling inside, it is time to execute on the path ahead. The first order of business in carrying out a rescue is to make changes manageable. It is not the time or moment for grand visions.

In 1993, mainframe computer giant IBM was near collapse. Sales and profits were declining, market share eroding, and no one wanted the job as IBM's CEO. The *Fortune* 500 Goliath had lost touch with customers, was unable to bring scientific discoveries to market, and had erroneously dismissed the revolutionary impact of personal computing. IBM was considered a dinosaur by those inside and outside its industry.

IBM's reputation rescue began in 1993 when Lou Gerstner was named IBM's chairman and CEO. He focused IBM on solutions and action, proposing five specific priorities for the first 90 days of his leadership.[63] These five action steps steered the organization toward what had to be done:

1. Stop hemorrhaging cash. We were precariously close to running out of money.
2. Make sure we would be profitable in 1994 to send a message to the world—and to the IBM workforce—that we had stabilized the company.
3. Develop and implement a key customer strategy for 1993 and 1994 —one that would convince customers that we were back serving their interests, not just pushing "iron" (mainframes) down their throats to ease our short-term financial pressures.
4. Finish right-sizing by the beginning of the third quarter.
5. Develop an intermediate-term business strategy.[64]

Gerstner understood that IBM had no choice but to make things happen. There was no time left for excuses or long-term visions. Instead, IBM needed to set a plan in motion that had clear, quantifiable goals. In *Who Says Elephants Can't Dance?* Gerstner wrote that IBM had to stop looking to blame others and tweaking the internal structures. It needed to break the reputation rescue phase into attainable pieces that IBM employees could follow.

Once a plan identifies what can be accomplished in 90 days, 120 days, or 180 days, the rescue or transformation process can began. Without set deliverables and actionable strategies, companies will not be able to set momentum in place and will lose sight of the light shining at the end of the tunnel.

Check Who and What Is Missing

In the rush of events when a crisis strikes, key stakeholders can go accidentally unnoticed. When former CEO Harry Stonecipher took charge of Boeing after a bidding scandal, he made it clear that he would be meeting with key people in Washington, D.C. to make amends for various Defense Department scandals. As previously discussed in this chapter, leaders must keep an eye out on employees so that their companies' hard-won customer base is not sacrificed because of preoccupation with the crisis. A corporation has to deal with a crisis, but the core business must not languish. The key players in that business—whether it be Wall Street, top customers, regulators, or media—cannot be ignored. Someone has to be minding the store.

Nor should company principles and values be allowed to deteriorate due to upper management's being consumed with crisis matters. The unhinging of a company, even the venerable *New York Times*, can easily happen when no one is looking. As reported by Kurt Andersen in *New York* magazine, the *New York Times* management was so preoccupied with reporter Jayson Blair's fabricated story and missteps by Executive Editor Howell Raines that they did not properly supervise reporter Judith Miller's interviews with top White House aides over the leaking of undercover CIA agent Valerie Plame Wilson's name. "In other words, during the very period when free-ranging Judy Miller desperately needed adult supervision—when she was publishing another half-dozen exciting stories about the discovery of Iraqi WMDs, when she was having all her conversations with Libby et al. about Plame and Wilson—her senior management was entirely consumed by the Raines-Blair horror show."[65]

Management must be careful not to let tunnel vision set in. The show must go on. Critics are waiting in the wings to write their critiques, and rave reviews are needed to fill seats on night two.

CONCLUSION

Now that the first several steps to recovery are under way, the next phase of restoring reputation requires taking stock of how the company lost its footing in the first place. Following the steps outlined in this Rescue chapter should leave employees and leaders feeling somewhat more confident that better days lie ahead. They have taken the heat, communicated untiringly, settled on priorities for the next 90 days, and are keeping an eye out for stinging punches from competitors and critics.

CHAPTER 5

REWIND

"We had to settle with the past to prepare the future."

—Carlos Ghosn, CEO, Nissan[1]

"It was operating too close to too many margins."

—Harold W. Gehman Jr., Columbia Shuttle Accident Investigation Board
Chairman[2]

On February 1, 2003, the world learned that the space shuttle *Columbia* burst into flames just moments before its reentry into the earth's atmosphere. The explosion killed all seven astronauts on board and rained debris from Texas to Louisiana. The American public mourned as memories of the 1986 *Challenger* shuttle explosion came rushing back. Since the rocket had already survived takeoff, the most dangerous phase of its 16-day mission, the *Columbia* shuttle disaster caught everyone by surprise. National Aeronautics and Space Administration (NASA) officials promised the public a complete investigation to determine the blast's cause.

Ninety-one minutes after the *Columbia* exploded, NASA activated its internal Headquarters Contingency Action Team and the external International Space Station and Space Shuttle Mishap Interagency Investigation Board. The independent board's mission was to uncover all the facts related to the explosion and recommend preventative actions.

Retired Navy Admiral Harold W. Gehman Jr. was chosen as the board's lead independent panel investigator. Gehman had served as commander in chief of the U.S. Joint Forces Command and co-chairman of the Department of Defense review of the *USS Cole* terrorist bombing. The board immediately began work at Barksdale Air Force Base in Louisiana on the evening following the blast.[3]

From the beginning, the board set several far-reaching demands:[4]

- Establish an office physically outside of NASA headquarters in order to separate its activities from the internal investigation.
- Revise the charter on roles and responsibilities to ensure greater independence from NASA. The revisions included:
  - Hiring its own administrative and technical staff to test and analyze the data.
  - Acquiring its own independent budget.
  - Giving Board Chairman Gehman absolute authority to appoint new board members.
  - Providing detailed and full progress reports to the public through frequent press briefings.
  - Agreeing to issue the final report at the same time to all constituencies.
  - Offering the option of minority reports for board members who disagreed with any of the findings.
- Bring in additional board members who had the expertise needed for the investigation.
- Divide the 13-member board into four groups to oversee key investigatory areas:
  - NASA management and materials care, and shuttle maintenance safety.
  - NASA training, and operation and in-flight performance of ground and shuttle crews.
  - Engineering and technical analysis.
  - NASA history, budget, and institutional culture and its effect on the shuttle program.

- Review lessons from the 1986 *Challenger* and 1967 *Apollo* fire accidents as well as best practices from three independent safety programs that have near-perfect, accident-free performance.
- Build its own web site (www.caib.us) for board biographies, press briefings, public input, and the final report.
- Establish a process for gathering and tracking all public input, that is, a 24-hour hotline, mailing addresses, and a web site for online comments to allow submission of photographs, comments, and technical papers, among other materials and information.
- Use a separate database server from NASA to maintain security.
- Upgrade the database, software, and information management systems.

Seven months later, the *Columbia* accident board issued an 11-volume report at a nationwide press briefing. The investigation concluded that one-half of the shuttle's failure was due to aerodynamics and the other half was due to a breakdown in leadership. According to the report, "In the Board's view, NASA's organizational culture and structure had as much to do with this accident as the External Tank foam."[5] The board did not like what it had learned about the NASA culture.

> The organizational causes of this accident are rooted in the Space Shuttle Program's history and culture, including the original compromises that were required to gain approval for the Shuttle Program, subsequent years of resource constraints, fluctuating priorities, schedule pressures, mischaracterizations of the Shuttle as operational rather than developmental, and lack of an agreed national vision. Cultural traits and organizational practices detrimental to safety and reliability were allowed to develop, including: reliance on past success as a substitute for sound engineering practices (such as testing to understand why systems were not performing in accordance with requirements/specifications); organizational barriers which prevented effective communication of critical safety information and stifled professional differences of opinion; lack of integrated management across program elements; and the evolution of an informal chain of command and decision-making processes that operated outside the organization's rules.[6]

In short, the board declared that NASA was not a learning organization. First, the space organization had not effectively heeded lessons from the *Challenger* debacle two decades earlier. Second, management made decisions with little input and did not value dissenting views. Engineers' opinions were ignored. As written in the report, "Managers' claims that they didn't hear the engineers' concerns were due in part to their not asking or listening."[7] Authority was based on seniority and desk location. Third, mistakes were hidden, and the preferred mode of Power-Point presentations often masked critical details that led to flawed analyses. Fourth, and equally unsettling, employees believed that if they could outwait leadership changes, they could get back to doing things the way they used to.[8] Speaking at a Wharton Leadership Conference in June 2002, Admiral Gehman said that politics overrode intelligence in NASA's informal chain of command and decision making.

The external board's conclusions about NASA's ineffectual culture and leadership hold profound lessons for all modern organizations looking to understand organizational failure. Its leadership had unintentionally created blind spots and would say one thing but behave the opposite way. As Admiral Gehman remarked:

> I mean I'll give you a case in point. If—if you have a—if you say that safety is the most important trait and characteristic of this organization, but then you require a person who's in charge of some program to come and travel to your office every month and report on how the schedule's coming, well you're saying one thing and you're sending another message.[9]

In NASA's defense, the organization functioned under severe operational and budgetary restraints. The *Columbia* space shuttle program faced outdated technologies, inadequate technical oversight, flight scheduling pressures, staff reductions, insufficiently trained personnel, poor intrateam communications, and a lack of checks and balances. Not surprisingly, many companies would admit to limitations similar to those experienced by NASA.

In reality, the obstacles and budgetary constraints facing NASA and now all organizations will only increase in the years ahead as they strive to be as lean as possible. Nevertheless, the lessons from the *Columbia* shuttle tragedy should reinforce leaders' determination to carefully learn from the past because the cost of failing to do so far exceeds the cost of doing so.

This part of the Reputation Recovery model—Rewind—describes how troubled companies should turn back the clock, even momentarily, to review what went wrong in order to prevent any additional injuries to their reputations, and move forward. Nevertheless, not every company takes the time to look in the rearview mirror. This chapter also calls for the importance of developing baseline measures from which to gauge recovery's momentum and progress.

STEP 5: ANALYZE WHAT WENT WRONG *AND* RIGHT

As soon as leaders sense that they have stabilized or rescued their company's reputations from the grip of destruction, they should step back and start asking questions. By studying one's own mistakes and those of others, companies can avoid repeating or encountering even larger problems that may lie ahead.

During Xerox's Rewind phase, CEO Anne Mulcahy rewound the clock to make sure that the same mistakes were never repeated at the document company. While talking to a Texas customer, the customer remarked that Mulcahy was "like the farmer whose cow was stuck in the ditch." When Mulcahy look puzzled by this colloquial expression, he explained that much like her company, she had to understand how the cow got in the ditch in the first place to ensure that the cow never fell into that trench again.[10]

The Xerox CEO gladly followed his advice. After careful analysis of what Xerox had done wrong, Mulcahy identified three remedies to help lift Xerox out of its own ditch—fewer ill-considered restructurings, less fearful work environment, and a common set of objectives.[11] Armed with the knowledge of past mistakes, the new CEO was able to intelligently repair Xerox's reputation and create a viable future.

When Tyco International's new CEO Ed Breen took over from ousted CEO Dennis Kozlowski, Breen took swift action by firing 290 of Tyco's top 300 executives and handing out pink slips to the entire board.

To build the "different"[12] company he hoped to shape, Breen looked to Tyco's past for lessons learned. He requested a "root-cause analysis" (RCA) to determine how the *Fortune* 500 company got itself into its deep financial difficulties and what could be done to prevent them from happening again.[13] RCA is based on the assumption that problems are best solved by attempting to correct or eliminate underlying causes rather than merely addressing the symptoms and repairing any damage. By directing corrective measures at root causes, companies can minimize the problem's recurrence over the long term.

In search of the origins of BP's overall reputation collapse, Lord Browne drilled deep into BP's history. In a *Fortune* interview,[14] Browne remarked that the company needed to investigate why problems did not surface sooner. The beleaguered CEO and U.S. senior executive team appointed external experts to assess what failed them. An external team assured independence and guaranteed transparency.

Other institutions like Xerox and BP do not shy away from revisiting the past to create a better future. The National Transportation Safety Board (NTSB) investigates airline crashes and other transportation accidents with a primary focus on finding the cause—not who is at fault. Hospitals now hold "mortality and morbidity" conferences to better understand medical errors and prevention. The Army's "After-Action Reviews" study what happened in battle and reasons behind large and small judgment errors. These nearly routine reviews by *Fortune* 500 companies, the NTSB, hospitals, and the Army are not meant primarily as critiques but as forums for learning lessons, gathering information, and establishing better controls to prevent future crises from occurring and be better prepared should a crisis arise.

Factiva and other information resource companies can provide a look in the rearview mirror. These companies are important resources to review media coverage that occurred several months before the crisis and pinpoint any critical warning signs that may have been overlooked. "Retromining" is another way to help companies determine if those telltale signs were possible to detect in the first place, or how far back they really existed. Companies that reflect on what happened to cause reputational harm can only be prepared for future troubling patterns.

During the Rewind stage of safeguarding and recovering reputation, companies should also carefully examine what they did *right* as well as wrong. It is easier for employees to accept change if they are presented with positive and negative information. For instance, the CEO of a global *Fortune* 500 subsidiary was fine-tuning his year-end address to top managers for their annual retreat. His presentation began with a historical look at how the team missed targets and underestimated its competitive challenges. An outsider pointed out that the CEO's message might be better received if he also mentioned what had gone better than expected during the prior year. The CEO took this advice and reported back that the balanced history ignited the team's enthusiasm to overcome its lackluster performance from the year before.

Not all CEOs look backward. Outsider CEOs brought in to save companies on life support often have too many fires to put out and too little time to focus on the past. IBM's turnaround CEO Lou Gerstner is often cited as the poster boy for this situation. When he began IBM's recovery, Gerstner said that the technology giant needed to set its sights on future solutions rather than past problems.

Similar to Gerstner, McKesson CEO John Hammergren had no time to dwell on the past at the fallen health care information and services company: "But I spent most of my time focused on going forward rather than trying to understand what had happened in the past. . . . It was one thing to discover what had happened and why, and another thing to have a company going forward. So my mission, my first priority, became to gather people up off the floor and to focus them on what needed to be done to make things right."[15]

Resistance to investigating past, present, or future problems is not uncommon. According to Stanford University professor Robert Proctor, "There is a lot more protectiveness than there used to be. It is often safer not to know."[16] Due to an increasing prevalence of not wanting to know all the facts, Dr. Proctor has launched an entirely new approach to the study of ignorance called *agnotology*. A clear example of an agnotologian is the late

Enron Chairman Ken Lay, who ignored early warning signals from whistle-blower Sherron Watkins about the company's pending financial collapse.

Not studying failure can be costly. Professors Mark Cannon and Amy Edmondson of Harvard Business School examined why some companies fail to learn and subsequently learn to fail.[17] They argue that it is only natural for employees or leaders to ignore or deny failure. People fear for their jobs and can be blind to their own deficiencies. However, Cannon and Edmondson highlight the extreme risk that companies take when they overlook judgment errors of all sizes or "near misses" that can ultimately wreak havoc. They believe that companies that reinforce identifying their mistakes and learning from them are steps ahead of catastrophic failure. Looking backward, even for just a moment, can be preventative medicine.

Every leader is different about how much time he thinks he has to right the ship after reputation has been lost. Depending on the urgency of the situation, there may, in fact, be no time to identify the root causes for reputation erosion. However, companies should carve out time to isolate the factors that brought them to where they are so that they can rebuild enduring and lasting reputations. Furthermore, an analysis of what went wrong, and hopefully what went right, is invaluable for measuring long-term progress, establishing metrics, and achieving closure on an unpleasant chapter in a company's history.

Establish a Task Force

With great frequency, companies and institutions are establishing task forces to identify the fault lines that existed before all systems failed. These task forces are triggered when organizations fail and stakeholders demand an account of what went wrong. As the NASA example underscored, internal and external independent teams were quickly called into action to determine the causes of the *Columbia* shuttle explosion.

The *New York Times*'s use of an internal task force after the Jayson Blair scandal is another example of the positive impact an independent investigation can have. As an internal report noted: "The shock to our system—to its morale and reputation—has created an important opportunity. Most important, it has created a consensus for change."[18]

To uncover the changes needed to return the influential paper's reputation to its premier status, the *New York Times* announced the formation of a task force to investigate the newsroom's hiring, management, and fact-checking practices and uncover how Blair's plagiarism continued unnoticed for so long.[19] The task force, led by Assistant Managing Editor Allan Siegal, consisted of 22 internal *Times* staffers and three independent outsiders. When the Siegal Report was issued, it was clear that nothing was off limits. The task force went as far as criticizing Executive Editor Howell Raines's condoned favoritism and management style. He was singled out for allowing a culture that enabled Blair's fabrications. Raines eventually lost his job in the scandal's wake.

The *Times*'s task force recommended two calls to action:

1. Creation of a public editor or ombudsman to represent readers' interests and the paper's editorial practices.
2. A newly created masthead role responsible for publication standards and compliance; and a second masthead position responsible for hiring, promotions, staffing, and career development.[20]

Newly hired Executive Editor Bill Keller endorsed the depth and breadth of the Siegal Report. He was thankful that he could begin his plan of action to restore the *Times*'s reputation for credibility instead of spending his early reign assessing the damage. As Keller responded, "While there is little in this independent analysis to make us proud, I am proud that we began the process of restoring order by facing our failures squarely."[21] For Keller, the Siegal Report put to bed lingering questions concerning the incident and follow-up investigation, and served as a road map for what not to repeat as he took charge.

Nearly one year later, a second Siegal internal task force was finding ways to further strengthen the newspaper's credibility and trust.[22] The committee of 19 internal news staff reviewed the paper's strategies for reaching out to readers and an increasing wave of critics. The group concluded that the *Times* was not safeguarding its reputation:

> In today's media environment, such a minimal response [to critics] damages our credibility. Critics, competitors and partisans can too easily caricature who we are and what we do. And loyal readers gain no solid understanding of what the truth really is. Therefore we need to be more assertive about explaining ourselves—our decisions, our methods, our values, how we operate.[23]

By instituting a second internal review of ongoing challenges, the *Times* again corrected its course of action and remained hard at work healing its bruised reputation.

Near the third anniversary of the Blair incident, the *Times*'s Public Editor Byron Calame asked Siegal Report members to consider whether another Blair-like fiasco could occur. Besides the few maybes, answers to Calame's "rewind" question yielded a vote of confidence. For the most part, members believed that safeguards recommended by the previous task forces were working. Yet, Calame wisely pointed out that, "While procedural safeguards can be cranked up fairly quickly, altering the culture of the newsroom is a longer-term proposition."[24] Without a doubt, culture change is the most difficult part of restoring long-term reputation and is addressed more fully in Chapter 6.

Identify Distress Signals: Keep Antennae Alert

Reputations are not destroyed overnight, but are gradually worn down over time, with the collective impact of each incident further chipping away at the company's reputational foundation. What this means for leaders is that if they could identify the telltale warning signs of impending reputation failure as they occur, they could take immediate steps to halt its progress. If BP had only heeded such signals and asked itself what danger signs had emerged that needed immediate attention, crisis could have been averted. The oil refinery's tragic explosion occurred only several weeks after a BP planning document identified the Texas City refinery as a top risk for the oil giant.[25]

When commenting on his resignation as top man at renowned investment bank Morgan Stanley, Phil Purcell spoke not of opportunity lost but of warnings missed. "It was many, many little waves," he said. "It wasn't one storm."[26] Purcell's comments mirror what is often heard from leaders presiding over a crisis. They admit that there were often clear and present warning signs—or little waves—that signaled that trouble was brewing. These signals are ignored because they either do not make their way to the corner office or are erroneously perceived as innocuous.

According to published reports, warning signs should have been evident to Purcell toward the end of his tenure at Morgan Stanley—top executives were bailing out, employees were openly criticizing the CEO to reporters, and customers were complaining of feeling unappreciated. The good news is that in corporate life, early detection can save a company's reputation.

Distress signals arrive in many forms and from a variety of sources. They can come from customers, employees, and other stakeholders. What they have in common is that they eventually surface, whether it is months or years before the actual crisis. One such example came from a money management firm that consistently told automotive interiors manufacturer Lear that it needed to refinance its debt while business was good. After repeated conversations, the money manager Rich Pzena went as far as writing a formal letter to Lear leadership.[27] Unfortunately, Lear discounted his entreaties, and the company paid the price by refinancing during downtimes.

In hindsight, careful screening for unusual patterns or irregularities would have quickly revealed that IBM was not in its best fiscal shape. When IBM's Lou Gerstner joined the failing computer company in 1993, he found 142 different European financial systems, 128 chief information officers, and 800 different logos.[28] Similarly, financial services juggernaut Merrill Lynch (also cynically referred to as Mother Merrill) had signs of deteriorating health. When newly instated CEO Stanley O'Neal took charge of the financial behemoth, he was described as "one of the few to recognize that Merrill had fattened itself for slaughter."[29] O'Neal's intense focus on trimming the fat is now part of Merrill Lynch's legendary success and recovery. Typical symptoms of clogged corporate arteries were also found in abundance at Motorola when new CEO Ed Zander took over. For Motorola, the corporate bloat was found at the top, requiring a careful thinning at the vice president level.[30]

It pays to watch for troubling signs. Listening could have helped automated cash machine manufacturer Diebold before storm clouds appeared and lightning struck. When Diebold decided to expand into automated touch-screen voting machines by purchasing Global Election Systems (GES), Diebold should have heeded the advice of skeptical computer scientists and voting-advocacy groups such as blackboxvoting.com. Consultancy Evolve24 also surfaced existing technical documents calling attention to GES's technological weaknesses.[31] These detractors raised questions about GES machines' tamper fallibility and ability to provide detailed audit logs.[32]

When media coverage eventually mushroomed over the machine's imperfections and some states rejected the machines, GES began to pay attention. Diebold's problems escalated when voter advocate Bev Harris reported online that some of GES's management had prior criminal records. Diebold's tidal wave of negative publicity might have been less severe if they had more finely tuned antennae that could have picked up this troubling information prior to the purchase.

Weber Shandwick's *Safeguarding Reputation* research found that blogs, wikis, social network spaces, and discussion boards are frequently home to distress signals, and should be closely monitored as part of a company's reputation management strategy. Ironically, only about one-third of global executives (31 percent) report that they pay a lot of attention to reputations online. North American executives are considerably less likely to monitor their company's reputation online compared with European and Asian executives (19 versus 32 versus 38 percent, respectively).[33]

An example of the need for online monitoring comes from a major computer company. A top executive was named in local newspapers for a misdemeanor as the company was facing intense scrutiny over financial irregularities. The local report reached a frequent company critic who tried spreading the embarrassing news via his blog. When the executive was not dismissed, several dozen employees posted their complaints on the critic's blog.

Since the company had been regularly monitoring online conversations, it was able to quickly contain the situation by responding with an explanatory CEO statement to employees with relevant information that essentially quashed further criticism. As employees and stakeholders flock to the Web, knowledge of all types of online and offline company reputation busters becomes critical.

CEO Jonathan Carson of Nielsen BuzzMetrics states that "companies don't have to be held hostage by information out of their control, and they don't have to be the last to know."[34] By using brand-monitoring services that serve as consumer sentiment radar, companies can stay one step ahead of significant reputation damage. Carson gave the example of a telecom company whose reputation was severely tarnished by a "viral video" that spread like wildfire and hurt the brand's customer service reputation. Nielsen BuzzMetrics identified the video and alerted key managers within moments of its posting. They were able to instantly mobilize crisis-response efforts and implement strategies for various corporate departments, Web content managers, and marketing and operations officers.

Companies such as Nielsen BuzzMetrics are able to identify reputation threats emerging from tens of millions of blogs and other influential consumer-generated sources. As Carson sees it, "The environment of influence today is far more complex, dynamic and time-sensitive than ever before, and reputation threats move faster and strike harder."[35] Being alert to early warning signs or risks before a reputational crash is no longer a luxury, but a necessity.

Increasingly, more companies are building systems to capture early warning signs. Some companies depend on outside Internet monitoring vendors or engage in scenario planning to prepare for the unimaginable. Reputation dashboards can help provide information on emerging threats; however, companies should regularly practice how they would respond to problems if they arose. Once these plans are rehearsed and assessed for effectiveness, companies will be familiar with what their options are if a real threat arises.

If food companies had more carefully followed the obesity issue in the mid-1990s, they would not have been caught flat-footed when the issue exploded in public view. Similarly, if the FBI had heeded Minneapolis

Field Agent Coleen Rowley's request to obtain a warrant to wiretap and search the computer of September 11 terrorist Zacarias Moussaoui, the horrific tragedy may have taken a different course. Early detection rewards companies as well. Toyota launched its successful hybrid Prius automobile because of its inspection of societal shifts that revealed that consumers were concerned about carbon emissions and rising gas costs.

Early warning signs should be taken seriously. Once companies look back at the signals they missed, they can ensure that precautions are taken not to miss them again.

Find Your Beacons of Light

Many scandal-ridden companies soon learn that there are frequent unpleasant surprises on the long path to recovery. Waves of bad news can wash over companies and drown out any progress being made. Overcoming these gut-wrenching squalls is easier said than done. Boards and peers should encourage leaders to find their buoys in the storm. CEOs should seek out sounding boards that can easily look back at what they learned from confronting the demons of reputation failure and what they would have done differently. These beacons of light can guide companies to a safe landing when storm clouds darken the sky.

When new CEO John Swainson arrived to resuscitate the reputation of software maker Computer Associates (CA) after a series of scandals, he turned to several peers who had mastered the art of the turnaround. He spoke with Tyco's CEO Ed Breen and MCI's CEO Michael Capellas. Breen and Capellas underscored the importance of communications and patience in restoring CA's tarnished reputation. Swainson took to heart their advice that recovery takes more than one year and could possibly take as long as five years. He concluded: "It took a long time for CA to get so screwed up. It will take a long time to get it unscrewed up, and it will take even longer for people to recognize it."[36] To maintain perspective and overcome doubt, company leaders need to find safe harbors—fellow CEOs, advisers, loyal customers, trusted board members, or retired CEOs with seasoned backgrounds—during recovery's tough days and nights.

Customer advisory panels or individuals can help shine light on what went wrong to cause a misguided company to stumble. One besieged *Fortune* 500 institution with a powerful Asian subsidiary approached its recovery process by seeking out local market and customer insights. To start, the American-born CEO identified the region's 50 most influential customers whose support would be critical to resuscitating its reputation. Given the cultural and natural reticence of associating with a disgraced company, many key customers declined having their good names tied to the tarnished company. The CEO wisely accepted customers' concerns that were rooted in local custom and instead began gradually building one-on-one relationships with these key influencers.

Although the recovery process was now prolonged, the regional CEO received candid feedback during these individual meetings about how the company could reposition itself and mend its broken reputation. In time, the company rebuilt its standing, and the CEO now has a vast network of influentials to support the company as it grows.

Customers can not only serve as support for beleaguered leaders, but also provide them with information that may not have otherwise reached their ears. Sony CEO Howard Stringer confessed that he first heard about the enormity of the overheating computer battery problems from Dell's CEO Michael Dell.[37] Clearly, the distress signals at Stringer's own company had not rung loud enough to reach him.

Leaders should welcome bearers of bad news as enthusiastically as bearers of good news while they struggle to right their company's reputation. Every leader should have a customer like Michael Dell who forces companies to take off their blinders. As Sony management looks back at how they missed the magnitude of the battery problem, they will certainly weigh their risks more carefully.

A company's beacon could even be found a few levels below the chief executive. One large-sized company CEO looked to his top human relations officer for guidance and coaching on reviving his damaged personal reputation that had also negatively impacted the company's reputation. The human relations officer accompanied the CEO to town meetings where employees asked tough questions. Armed with sound advice on being contrite and humble, the CEO was overwhelmingly embraced by employees. He was glad he had not followed his natural inclination to explain the questionable ethical lapse in minute detail. For this particular CEO, the human relations executive's counsel helped him do what was right for the company and demonstrate that even CEOs can make foolish mistakes.

Advisers can provide critical input to the recovery process. Knowing that others have been through similar perfect storms shows companies and their leaders that they are not alone, that recovery pangs are normal, and that with clear directions, they can navigate their way back to higher ground. Beacons of light serve as rays of hope that are sorely needed during times of company turmoil.

STEP 6: MEASURE, MEASURE, AND MEASURE AGAIN

Now that the past is in full view, measurement can begin. To track progress once reputation loss has occurred, benchmarks are necessary. Now more than ever, companies and their leaders need real-time, hard evidence that the company is moving in the right direction.

According to reputation expert Joy Marie Sever, reputation measurement takes courage. Often, companies do not like what they hear. When they discover a problem exists, they must do something to remedy it.[38] The good news is that reputation measurement builds confidence. It takes away the mystery and uncertainties that may have been clouding a situation. Sometimes, knowledge reveals that a situation is not as dire as was originally thought, though usually it's a much-needed wake-up call. Either way, leaders know what they are dealing with and have the information needed to bring about change. Sever says: "They have quantified the unknown, and it is far easier to deal with the tangible than the elusive."[39]

Experts are right when they say you can manage only what you measure. Fewer than half of all companies have ongoing reputation management programs in place.[40] Reputation-tracking surveys should be conducted annually for the vast majority of companies, regardless of whether they are in crisis.

Companies whose reputations are under threat should initiate ongoing quarterly or half-yearly research. Without knowing what key stakeholders actually think of a company at multiple points in time, any progress in safeguarding or restoring a company's good name becomes dangerously dependent on anecdotes, media coverage, and hearsay. To find those hard-to-reach stakeholders such as financial analysts, regulators, journalists, key customers, and opinion leaders, in-depth qualitative interviews or "soft soundings" are best.

Companies should hire independent market research firms that have strong reputations for rigorous qualitative and quantitative research. Importantly, the chosen research firm should have no stake in the survey's outcome. Before meeting with qualified research firms to begin regularly tracking company perceptions, companies should ask themselves 15 basic questions and look to their research partners for help in answering them:

1. What are our business goals?
2. Who are our most important stakeholders (online and offline)?
3. Which competitors do we want to measure ourselves against?
4. What do we want stakeholders to believe about us?
5. What do stakeholders believe about us now?
6. What did stakeholders believe about us before the crisis?
7. What is the gap between how we want to be perceived and how we are perceived now?
8. What do we want stakeholders to do in support of our goals (e.g., buy stock, purchase products/services, apply for jobs, visit our web site for news, spread word-of-mouth, give us the benefit of the doubt)?
9. How do we communicate with internal and external stakeholders?
10. Which of our messages resonant and are credible (internally and externally)? Which messages need clarification, amplification, or adjustment? How would our competitors answer these questions?
11. How do stakeholders learn about us? Which sources are most believable and trusted?

12. Who is in charge of reputation management within our organization? Who should be in charge?

13. Which publicly available reputation scorecards are we winning? Not winning?

14. Which research milestones do we want to set for the next 6, 12, 18, and 24 months? What measures will we accept as success and as failure?

15. How can the research results best be used to advance strategy and be actionable?

Although the best research methodology provides consistent measurement across a wide spectrum of key stakeholders, companies should not ignore internal research already in place such as employee and customer satisfaction surveys. Companies often have untapped goldmines of research available. It is not uncommon for companies to ask their research groups to look back at internal research data to determine whether early warning signs could have been detected.

Research was clearly on the mind of IBM's turnaround CEO Lou Gerstner when he arrived at the struggling giant. As he began restoring the technology company's once sterling reputation, the new CEO asked to see customer satisfaction study results for IBM products and services. The customer reports he received were all positive. When he inquired how customer ratings could be so positive when every other corporate yardstick was proving otherwise, the new CEO uncovered disturbing news. The customer satisfaction survey sample was based on salespeople's recommended client names, not a statistically valid random sample.[41] This discovery explained why customer satisfaction scores were so high—for good reason, salespeople did not provide the names of dissatisfied customers!

Upon further inquiries into IBM benchmarking, Gerstner learned that there were 339 different satisfaction surveys, each with different methodologies, samples, and questions. IBM subsequently narrowed the number of surveys down to 14 and enlisted the help of an independent research firm. Soon, IBM was annually surveying over 100,000 customers and noncustomers in 30 languages in 55 countries. The recovering Goliath could now manage its progress with the proper baselines and could detect any underlying problems in their earliest stages.

Companies should not isolate measurement and perception in one corner of the company. The information should be shared and discussed broadly. For example, one *Fortune* 500 company holds a yearly reputation summit among division heads and lead directors to review the company's standing among key stakeholders and develop strategies for changing misperceptions.

Another company launched a reputation management council consisting of cross-unit division heads to meet quarterly with the communications council primarily responsible for reputation strategies and activities. The unit heads and communications professionals keep each other informed of any emerging issues that could threaten their reputation-rebuilding efforts. These companies reinforce the message that safeguarding reputation is everyone's business.

In addition to quantitative and qualitative research such as surveys and focus groups, daily media alerts are highly recommended for monitoring potential future problems and gauging public sentiment. These "early bird" alerts also come in handy when a company needs to look backwards during the Rewind phase. They should include intelligence on competitors, which allows the company to assess whether issues affecting competitors' reputations might spread cross-industry. One of the greatest shifts in the reputation landscape is how entire industries are now affected by the actions of only one or two companies. Keeping an eye on your competitors and industry is now required to monitor reputation threats.

Although many *Fortune* 500 companies already receive quarterly or yearly media audits from their communications departments or public relations agencies, crises and crises in the making now necessitate vigilant attention to online coverage, tonality, and conversation. Many new online services have surfaced to help companies and individuals monitor and manage their reputations online. These new tools provide invaluable information that search engines and Factiva searches cannot keep pace with.

Industry analyst firm Forrester gives several services high ratings for their brand monitoring—Nielsen BuzzMetrics, Biz360, and Cymfony.[42] Since Technorati estimates that nearly 175,000 new blogs and 1.6 million new posts are created every day,[43] companies cannot expect to keep up to date with what is being said about them by relying solely on standard search engines or quarterly reports.

Brand Association Mapping, a new product developed by Nielsen BuzzMetrics, is shown in Exhibit 5.1. For Nike, a full understanding of the "buzz" or conversation surrounding its brand reputation is displayed by frequency and strength of online commentary or associations. Using this type of visual display, Nike is able to assess which terms are most frequently used when discussing its brand. In this example, shoes and Adidas surface most often. Tellingly, sweatshop perceptions fall into a second order of conversations indicating that Nike, for the most part, has handled its earlier crises over sweatshop perceptions well. When a

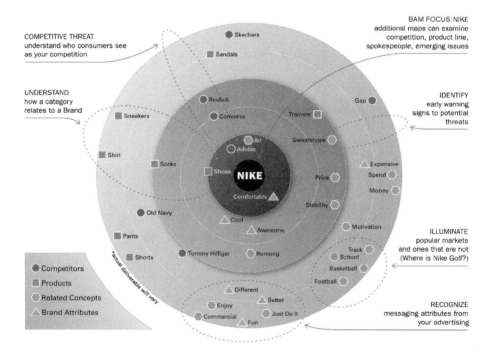

EXHIBIT 5.1   *Brand Mapping of Buzz*

Source: Nielsen BuzzMetrics.

company is in crisis mode or lifting itself out from under the weight of its troubles, brand association mapping provides real-time insights into how the brand is faring among the chatter. The map's information can help direct future marketing and communications efforts, and provide a window into what needs correcting.

Companies can also track their reputation progress by making use of publicly available and research-based reputation scorecards or league tables. Scorecard rankings serve as yardsticks for measuring reputation today. Now that the company is taking a deep breath to look around, it is the time to begin identifying the scorecards to apply for and set its sights on winning the best ones.

Making these "best of" lists can help dampen detractors' perceptions and boost employee motivation. For example, a leading company that had dropped several rankings in *Fortune's* America's and World's Most Admired Companies survey achieved a milestone for itself when it rebounded to make its industry's top-tier ranking over a two-year period.

Another smart way to learn from past mistakes is to initiate research on companies' best and worst reputation recovery practices. One global *Fortune* 50 company commissioned an in-depth best practices analysis of five reputation recoverers and five reputation sustainers to use as a road map for helping them overcome reputation damage. The deep analysis was pared down to 10 lessons that were eventually distributed to top management.

As sources of information proliferate and the business landscape rapidly changes, companies should also include in their study of best practices how to effectively use new media to restore their reputations. When JetBlue's CEO David Neeleman apologized to customers over February 2007 delayed flights, he placed his apology video on YouTube. One month later, YouTube reported 275,000 viewings of Neeleman's mea culpa.

Despite today's focus on metrics, it is important to note that measurement does not replace first-rate leadership and management, and an engaged culture. Numbers are important, but it is what leaders do with these numbers that counts most. Results should be incorporated into daily strategic and tactical plans for moving to the next phase of reputation recovery—restoring one's good name.

CONCLUSION

Looking back at how reputation risk could have been better managed and setting measurement systems in place provide the proper grounding for reviving reputation. The next chapter on restoring reputation begins the hard work of culture change, smart communications, and open dialogue.

CHAPTER 6

RESTORE

"As demoralizing as a slide down may be, the ride back up is infinitely more exhilarating."

—Alan Mulally, CEO, Ford Motor Company[1]

"History illustrates time and time again, that when the war is over the peace is more difficult to achieve."

—Fiona Colquhoun, Nonexecutive director of the Danish Leadership Institute[2]

Reaching this stage in the recovery continuum appears like a dream. The flashbacks of earlier days and nights are receding, although it is still hard for most leaders not to wake up in a cold sweat. All vital signs point to a return to health, and the company begins to take more secure steps. Despite looking forward to this day for the longest time, there are no parades being held or balloons taking flight as the company leaves the emergency room and gets back to business. Although the past several months have drained the organization and its leadership, restoring reputation requires its own sweat and tears.

Several years ago, Boeing found itself in need of reputation restoration. Even today, when "Boeing reputation" is searched in Google, nearly all top 20 mentions are related to scandals and reputation damage—"Ethics Expert Says Boeing Did the Right Thing," "Boeing's CEO Steps Down Amid Scandal," "We're Cleaning Up Our Own House," and "Boeing:

What Really Happened." In a brief three-year period, the once-legendary aircraft manufacturer fell from its lofty perch to become an example of unethical behavior.

Starting in 2002, the U.S. Justice Department handed down a prison sentence to Boeing's then–Chief Financial Officer Michael Sears for allegedly breaking conflict-of-interest laws. Sears was recruiting the former Air Force Procurement Officer Darleen Druyan at the same time she was negotiating a $23.5 billion contract to buy 100 Boeing tanker aircrafts. As a result of the scandal, Chairman and CEO Phil Condit resigned.

Compounding this ethical lapse in 2005, Condit's well-regarded successor Harry Stonecipher was found to be having an affair with a female Boeing executive. The board quickly dismissed Stonecipher and publicly stated that the once-retired CEO's behavior was inconsistent with Boeing's code of conduct. Adding more fuel to the fire, archrival Airbus soon passed Boeing as the world's largest commercial airline manufacturer.

The sudden executive void left by Stonecipher's departure was soon filled by Boeing board member and former 3M CEO and GE jet engine business executive James McNerney. His mandate was clear—restore luster to the once-invincible aerospace giant. One year later, McNerney was on his way to restoring Boeing's iconic reputation. Underscoring McNerney's early signs of progress on its road to recovery, Boeing witnessed an increase in its industry ranking from third to first place in *Fortune*'s 2007 World's Most Admired Companies survey.[3] In addition, both Boeing's share price and orders for its first new aircraft in 10 years, the 787 Dreamliner, were on an upward course.

McNerney's strategy to restore Boeing's reputation began simply— righting the culture, identifying values, and asking the right questions. As the new CEO told *BusinessWeek*: "If we can get the values lined up with performance, then this is an absolutely unbeatable company."[4] McNerney moved quickly. He worked hard to put an end to a warring rivalry between Boeing and merged McDonnell Douglas managers. He rebuilt a compensation system that rewarded collaboration instead of maintaining a culture built on fiefdoms and intimidation. The new CEO forced adversarial and siloed divisions to work toward a shared business purpose—the customer. He encouraged managers to speak up when something was wrong rather than allow a code of silence and resentment to prevail. Furthermore, McNerney was a role model of desirable executive behavior by remembering people's names, eliminating corporate perks, and freely sharing ideas with direct reports and employees.[5]

McNerney listened carefully to Boeing's critics and eased years-long tensions that had been building among key stakeholders. Five months into his new job, McNerney negotiated pay increases for restless engineers, and in the process averted a massive walkout. He also worked hard to smooth over Washington, D.C., relationships that were damaged from the string of government scandals. To start anew and end investigations into illegally obtained documents from competitor Lockheed Martin, Boeing ultimately paid a $615 million penalty to the U.S. government. The fine was the largest penalty ever imposed on a military contractor for misconduct.

Considering Boeing's poor ethical conduct of previous years, McNerney took the biggest step by revamping company values. The new "Living Boeing Values" now includes eight ideals—leadership, integrity, quality, customer satisfaction, people working together, diverse and involved team, good corporate citizenship, and enhancing shareholder value.[6]

To underscore the significance of values in restoring Boeing's reputation, McNerney did the unforgettable. At his first management offsite, McNerney displayed two numbers on the screen. "These are not ZIP codes," he said.[7] The two strings of figures were the prison numbers of Sears and Druyan. Senior management quickly got the message that ethical behavior was going to be as critical to the bottom line as making the numbers at the newly led Boeing.

Additionally, Boeing entered the blogosphere in an effort to become more transparent and less secretive. The aerospace giant now has blogs about nonconfidential information on the testing of its new 777 aircraft—and its marketing and communications strategies. It is also earning reputation points for inviting commentary and criticism.

Boeing's work at restoring reputation illustrates many of the important steps described in this chapter. After several scandal-ridden years, the new leadership at Boeing righted the culture, restored values, hired right, engaged detractors, and further engaged supporters.

As the Boeing experience clearly shows, restoring reputation is particularly difficult, but it can be done. Leaders have to prove themselves every day to doubting audiences, both internal and external. There is no shortage of critics and pundits who relentlessly refer to the company's misdeeds and overlook significant progress. Yet, now that a company fully understands its reputational missteps, it is time to brush aside skepticism and disappointment and embrace the positive. This chapter describes the step-by-step process of getting companies off the ventilator and breathing on their own again.

STEP 7: RIGHT THE CULTURE

Most chroniclers of corporate failure will readily admit that the company's culture is what failed the organization in the first place and that the only way to ensure recovery is by altering the corporate culture. As Tenet Healthcare Corporation CEO Trevor Getter noted during the recovery period following company allegations of Medicare fraud and overbilling, "I hope we have changed the culture because ultimately your culture is your only protection."[8]

Lou Gerstner, the former CEO of IBM, feels no differently. The IBM recovery had the words *culture change* written all over it. Gerstner too realized that the clearest path to successful recovery was mending IBM's broken culture:

> Until I came to IBM, I probably would have told you that culture was just one among several important elements in any organization's makeup and success—along with vision, strategy, marketing, financials, and the like. I might have chronicled the positive and negative cultural attributes of my companies ("positive" and "negative" from the point of view of driving marketplace success). And I could have told you how I went about tapping into— or changing—those attributes. The descriptions would have been

accurate, but in one important respect I would have been wrong. I came to see, in my time at IBM, that culture isn't just one aspect of the game—it is the game. In the end, an organization is nothing more than the collective capacity of its people to create value.[9]

Only when employees believe that they have as much to gain as senior management and their voices are being heard just as clearly can this "collective capacity" unleash the passion to rally behind change. When leaders engage employees and offer them something that truly resonates with their desire to help, restoration can finally begin. If an organization is committed to its workforce and keeps them motivated, employees will know how to behave when no one is watching and go the extra mile to help return the company to its former glory. To accomplish this goal, companies can consider some of the well-planned best practices that follow.

Similar to Boeing, there were signs at Royal Dutch Shell that not all was right *before* its oil reserves were exposed as being dramatically less than reported. The *Wall Street Journal* exposed some of the fault lines in the oil giant's culture that they believed led to Shell's embarrassing deception.[10] *Journal* reporters described how the stately and conservative Anglo-Dutch giant went overboard practicing "New Age Management" in the 1990s. In an unusually personal culture, Shell employees were encouraged to reveal their innermost feelings and perform skits to pitch new ideas. Shell employees were described as joking that E&P stood for Excel and PowerPoint, not Exploration and Production.[11]

The seeds of unconventional thinking were strewn during these fateful years and helped foster a culture where employees accepted risk over restraint. Clearly, Shell's announcement that its reserves were underreported revealed management mores that allowed individuals to decide whether they were going to follow audit guidelines. In fact, Shell's board was one of the last to know what was happening. The oil major's managers followed an unwritten rule that they were never to go directly to board members with issues or problems.[12]

Under new leadership, Shell's culture is being revamped and progress now seems to be on track to protect it from further harm. Fortunately, some of the creativity, unfettered input, and good deeds remain, but they are now balanced with policies and procedures that ensure that the company does not lose sight of its future direction.

Make Recovery Values Based

Although a few individuals can usually be blamed when a company loses reputation, wrongdoing is frequently systemic. If the culture does not actually encourage misconduct, then it at least tolerates it. For example, Enron's unethical and "anything goes" behavior was shown to be pervasive. A culture of unaccountability and poor leadership was evident at the Federal Emergency Management Agency (FEMA) when Hurricane Katrina relief efforts were badly fumbled in 2005. Additionally, WorldCom top officers, accountants, and finance heads were not the only ones to help erase $3.9 billion from the bottom line. At the same time the company was imploding, WorldCom salespeople were under investigation for overpaid commissions.[13]

To right a company's culture and restore its reputation, top management must pay the utmost attention to its values system, and apply steady pressure to replacing values that are either wrong or no longer relevant. Following the financial accounting fraud that hit McKesson Corporation, CEO John Hammergren knew that he needed to instill a value-centered culture to restore stakeholders' confidence in management and its internal culture. The CEO designed a set of shared principles called ICARE (Integrity, Customers first, Accountability, Respect, and Excellence).[14]

This values-based call to action communicated how employees should act and behave on their long road to recovery and afterwards. ICARE gave employees and leaders a structure that guided their actions and was something in which they could believe.

Values-based leadership is increasingly important as companies learn that they are now living in glass houses. If employees can be mobilized to pay attention to company values as they do their jobs, reputation risk will be diminished.

Hire Right

Time and time again, restoring reputation comes down to identifying the right people and putting them in charge. Enron is an example of what can happen to a well-regarded company when the wrong people are at the top. Senior Enron employees who should have served as role models for the next generation of leaders openly transgressed ethical boundaries and sent the message that work was all about the individual, not the team. Enron's policy to hire fast-track and overly aggressive business school graduates only exacerbated the underlying deceptive culture that already existed at the energy company.[15]

A company where people are hired only to push an agenda at all costs will suffer death of its reputation by a thousand cuts. By hiring the right people that set the right tone and share the right values, companies can avoid reputation failure, or at least mitigate its impact.

Returning to the Royal Dutch Shell example, there were many doubters when the company first hired Jeroen van der Veer as CEO. However, he has emerged as the right person at the right time and has succeeded in building a new winning culture. He has streamlined decision making and accountability.[16] Instead of downsizing as Shell did in the 1990s, the new CEO made a number of smart hires—4,500 mid-career professionals in 2006—and is filling the ranks with its first chief technology officer, seven chief scientists, and a climate control executive. The straight-talking CEO is a welcome departure from the company's early free-wheeling days.

Perhaps the best way to ensure that the most qualified people are populating a company's workforce is to train and groom them internally. For those companies trying to restore reputation, lessons can be learned from organizations whose reputations have been sustainable for the long term. GE's durable reputation can be attributed to its ability to build great leaders. Countless articles have been written about GE's people factory and subsequent success when GE leaders go on to lead other companies.

Similarly, HSBC has maintained its reputational equity by consistently promoting from within and diligently training its talent. HSBC refers to its talent philosophy as "growing its own timber." Toyota, another reputation sustainer, believes that its 250,000-employee workforce keeps its reputation strong by strictly adhering to the Toyota Way of consensus building and problem solving, and hiring with these values in mind. A common phrase heard at Toyota about its human resources practices is: "Before we build cars, we build people."[17]

Reaffirm People's Beliefs in Themselves

As the recovery process gathers steam, remaining employees have to be reassured that they have what it takes to make the company successful once again. With their confidence shaken, employees have to begin believing that what looks impossible is possible.

One way to build confidence back into a culture that has undergone extreme stress is to identify short-term wins that build momentum. Motorola's new CEO Ed Zander did just that when taking the helm at the then poorly performing and tired technology company. Zander saw his opportunity in the ultra-thin Razr cell phone and fast-tracked its development. Nine months later, Razr sales were skyrocketing and declared a hit. The new CEO was able to rally employees demotivated from years of declining share price, stunted technology advancements, and lackluster products.

With its confidence regained, the company was able to sprint past competitors and begin concentrating on a culture better suited to fast-paced technology. However, Motorola's upward reputation climb after Zander's arrival stumbled in 2007 when the prices of the popular Razr phone fell and its newer phones missed sales targets. Hard work now lies ahead, but at least employees saw that recovery is possible and experienced firsthand the taste of success. This brush with recovering its reputation might be enough to recapture momentum.

As Xerox CEO Anne Mulcahy demonstrated so dramatically, rebuilding confidence does not have to originate from current circumstances. She gathered key executives and asked them to envision an article written five years later on the company's triumphant recovery. Along with a plausible issue date, Mulcahy requested that the article include customer quotes, financial snapshots, and milestones. Looking back, CEO Mulcahy noted that "A lot of what we hoped might happen happened. Not everything. People actually ask me now, 'When is this going to happen?' You have to go, 'Hello . . . we made it up.' "[18] Similar to Motorola's sweet taste of success, once people envision that recovery is possible and own a piece of that hope, confidence has a good chance of returning and seeding a new culture.

CEO Trevor Fetter of Tenet Healthcare understood that management working together can recover together. In the third week of every month, Fetter instituted a three-day "no fly zone" where management had to be available for a team meeting. In addition, senior executives were moved to office space near their direct reports to establish ties and foster open communications. The CEO believed that unless senior managers spent time together, committed to one another, and had positive relationships with those under their supervision, the company would not be successful in returning to winning form.

To ensure that employees are sufficiently committed to rebuilding a sustainable culture, market researcher Gallup Organization developed a powerful tool that measures employee allegiance. Gallup developed 12 questions[19] (Q^{12}) to measure employee commitment levels and tied them to financial performance and growth. The 12 questions were built from hundreds of focus groups and employee interviews across diverse sectors and countries. The Q^{12} are described in Gallup partners Rodd Wagner and James Harter's book *12: The Elements of Great Managing*:[20]

1. I know what is expected of me at work.
2. I have the materials and equipment I need to do my work right.
3. At work, I have the opportunity to do what I do best every day.
4. In the last seven days, I have received recognition or praise for doing good work.
5. My supervisor, or someone at work, seems to care about me as a person.
6. There is someone at work who encourages my development.
7. At work, my opinions seem to count.
8. The mission or purpose of my company makes me feel my job is important.

9. My associates or fellow employees are committed to doing quality work.
10. I have a best friend at work.
11. In the last six months, someone at work has talked to me about my progress.
12. This last year, I have had opportunities at work to learn and grow.

When companies begin to recover from the reputation free fall that frequently precedes and follows crises, high levels of employee engagement are critical to survival. The Gallup authors report that "Ultimately, what emerged are the 12 elements of work life that define the unwritten social contract between employee and employer. Through their answers to the dozen most important questions and their daily actions that affected performance, the workers were saying, 'If you do these things for us, we will do what the company needs of us.'"[21]

Companies looking for employees to help them recover from reputation woes should be reminded that recovery is not possible until employees reach higher levels of satisfaction on the issues that are most important to them and are raised in these questions.

Identify Common Purpose and Values

Creating a team of engaged employees requires that they understand what is being asked of them. In short, leadership must be able to instill a common purpose that makes personal sacrifice meaningful during these dark days.

Office supply retailer Staples found itself in need of a reputational compass in 2002. Its North Star was finding a chief executive who could chart the right course and bring clarity to its clouded reputation. At the time, big-box office supply chains were seen as having limited future growth prospects. Staples, Office Depot, and OfficeMax had overexpanded and lacked differentiation. At Staples, a new CEO took over from founder Thomas Stemberg and proved the critics wrong. Ron Sargent, former chief operating officer (COO) of Staples, rose to the challenge by refocusing the company on the small-business customer.

"On my first day as CEO, I put on the black pants, black shoes, and red shirt that our associates wear and headed to our Brighton store. We opened the very first Staples store in Brighton, Massachusetts, in 1986, and by going there, I tried to rally the Staples troops around a concept that I call 'Back to Brighton.' It's a symbolic message to the members of our organization that we're going to improve service and refocus on our core customer base: the small-business customer."[22]

Sargent's clear-sightedness on returning Staples to its origins and finding its common purpose helped put the office supply company back on *BusinessWeek* 2004's 50 top-performing companies in America rankings.[23] The visible symbol of both the CEO and employees wearing aprons and working together was one surefire remedy for realizing the company's comeback and sending the message that a common goal had been found.

Although IBM was revived under former CEO Lou Gerstner, the hard work of finding its center of gravity was left to successor CEO Sam Palmisano. He realized that without shared principles and core beliefs, IBM could never truly be great again. IBM's workplace had changed since Gerstner's earlier reign—now nearly 40 percent of the workforce did not report into an IBM facility but worked on site at client facilities, from home, or when traveling. It was becoming more difficult to introduce values to a dispersed and partially faceless global culture.

In 2003, IBM held an online jam for its 320,000 employees that lasted 72 hours. Employees were encouraged to react honestly to a new set of IBM's principles that came from extensive employee focus groups and surveys. Some of IBM's older values set down by founder Thomas Watson Sr. that were no longer relevant were ultimately discarded and new ones were added. A revised set of corporate principles were chosen that carried meaning throughout the organization: Dedication to every client's success; Innovation that matters—for our company and for the world; and Trust and personal responsibility in all relationships.

Palmisano expects that this new IBM cultural revolution will take 10 to 15 years to take hold and will be the force that restores IBM to its former number-one position in the world. Palmisano says, "For one thing, people—rather than products—become our brand. Just as our products have had to be consistent with the IBM brand promise, now more than ever, so do our people."[24] In essence, Palmisano is assuring IBM's workforce that they are its brand, now and in the future, and will help create its everlasting reputational power.

Cultures are certainly not built overnight. However, cultures in crisis-ridden companies have to be attended to. A steady focus on values, talent, confidence, and a common purpose help provide a good running start in repairing reputation for the long term.

STEP 8: SEIZE THE SHIFT

After crisis strikes and the painful process of recovery begins, business models and practices often need changing. A surprising number of crises can be traced to shifts in the business climate that leaders did not see, ignored, or did not take seriously enough.

The classic case of a company's failure to recognize a business shift was IBM. IBM's bet on the staying power of the mainframe and overlooking the PC revolution resulted in the computer company's downhill slide in the early 1990s. The loss of sight surrounding the newly emerging PC business model was not surprising considering that IBM's System/360 mainframe business was breakthrough technology of its time. The System/360 was IBM's mainstay and cash cow for decades. As IBM's turnaround CEO Lou Gerstner described the mainframe business: "And the franchise was a gold mine. IBM's share of the computing market skyrocketed. Competitors reeled; many disappeared. The company's revenues grew at a compound growth rate of 14 percent from 1965 to 1985. Gross profit margins were amazing—consistently around 60 percent. Market share exceeded an astounding 30 percent, which eventually invited antitrust scrutiny."[25]

Who can blame IBMers for ignoring this business transformation when they held all the chips? Gerstner said that IBM's failure in the 1990s was not just that PCs were gaining ground, but also that IBM had not sized up this new market in time to develop an offensive strategy to challenge this mounting threat.[26] The PC challenge was already on the horizon, but IBM had its blinders on.

It is not uncommon for companies that find themselves caught in the undertow of change to suffer from "exceptionalism"—the belief that one's own industry is unique and unlike others. IBM had trouble imagining a world without the mainframe and had to quickly scramble to regain its prominence.

Pharmaceutical companies are another good example of an industry suffering from exceptionalism. The pharmaceutical industry's response to criticism about rising drug costs has been that they need to charge premium prices to pay for the research and development that fills their pipelines with new disease-curing drugs. As rational as this argument may be, all the general public sees is rising health care and drug costs.

The pharmaceutical industry has now awakened to the power of public opinion and to empowered patient and disease groups that have actively harmed its reputation. Although pharmaceutical companies had enjoyed positive perceptions among the general public for decades, Laura Schoen, Weber Shandwick's president of global health care, says, "Shifting public sentiment has changed the pharmaceutical industry dynamics forever and led it to acknowledge that it faces challenges similar to other scrutinized industries. The industry is no longer taking its reputation for granted."[27]

Another telling example of failing to consider the contextual business or shifting political environment before taking action comes from AT&T in 1996. The telecom giant announced the loss of 40,000 jobs as part of its restructuring under CEO Robert Allen. Like most job-elimination announcements, Wall Street welcomed the news and the company's market capitalization rose $6 billion in two days.[28] What AT&T did not realize was that this news would also be taken as an assault on the working class.

As AT&T's former Public Relations Officer Dick Martin explains in his book *Tough Calls*,[29] the layoff announcement came during Pat Buchanan's U.S. presidential primary campaign. Presidential hopeful

Buchanan used the layoffs as a symbol of corporate greed and further fueled the public's prevailing sense of economic uncertainty. The media soon jumped on the bandwagon, denouncing the profiteering of CEOs and decline of the middle class. The *New York Times* began a multiple series on downsizing, and *Business Week* issued an entire special issue on economic anxiety. The most memorable coverage sparked by the A&T announcement was *Newsweek*'s "Corporate Killers" cover with CEO photos looking like America's Most Wanted Criminals.

Despite even larger company layoffs than AT&T's, the entire country took the AT&T news personally, as though it were happening to them. Even U.S. Secretary of Labor Robert Reich joined the fray:

> Does a company have obligations and responsibilities beyond the bottom line? Does a company owe anything to its workers, its workers' families, the communities in which it does business? Managers who balk at executing the judgments of the market may fear with some reason that they will quickly face their own day of reckoning. And yet, I want to suggest to you that this restricted vision of stewardship may be ultimately disastrous for this country. And it may ultimately harm American business.[30]

Although AT&T leadership intended to generate positive news that it was taking care of business after its disastrous acquisition of NCR and well-documented runaway expenditures, the public was uneasy about the past recession and weakening employer-employee contract. Further inflaming the situation, CEO Allen's job layoff announcement was followed closely by news that he was granted $10 million in stock options.

A tempest was now raging. As Martin effectively describes the convergence of circumstances: "Incredibly, none of us at AT&T had connected the two events, largely because they had actually occurred months apart. The option grant had been made at the time of the company's restructuring announcement, months before the size of any downsizing was known. But their public release within days of each other was starkly insensitive."[31] Such notorious coverage and bad press may have been prevented if AT&T had had a better sense of public sentiment at the time of these dual announcements. However, as history has repeatedly shown, hindsight is always easier than foresight.

When confronted with restoring reputation, leaders need to be alert to small and large business shifts that can impact their future. If these changes are relevant—and they often are—reputation restoration should occur within the context of these seismic shifts. Several key questions that leaders should be asking themselves as they face a new future are:

- What are the biggest shifts in the world today? How do they affect us?
- Where will our industry be in the next two to three years? Who and what is driving our industry?
- What will be expected of leading companies in three years?
- What will customers need from us in three years?
- Where will we be in three years? What is stopping us from getting there? What should we be doing now?
- What threats will challenge our firm and industry over the next three years?
- What signals are weak but already on the horizon?
- Can we change the game? What game changer would propel us beyond all others?
- Will our answers to these questions astound competitors?
- Will our answers to these questions inspire our people, resonate with our customers, and capture the world's imagination?

Only by understanding and recognizing these business shifts will companies improve their chances of keeping the grim reaper away. When companies are in recovery mode, the answers to these questions can mean the difference between success, failure, and mediocrity.

Wal-Mart is a textbook case of a company late to realize that the ground has shifted dramatically beneath it. Nevertheless, Wal-Mart is also a case study of a company that addressed the changes they had previously ignored. The long-revered company quickly began to realize that its traditional way of doing business did not fit in with a growing public social consciousness. Once Wal-Mart's management realized that consumers expected more from companies than size and everyday low prices, Wal-Mart started down the path of embracing new business practices. It cannot be denied that the giant retailer has hit more than a few bumps in the road, but it would be nearly impossible not to notice the company's ongoing efforts to adapt to a new business reality.

Although Wal-Mart had always quietly supported educational initiatives in the communities where it operated, this number-one U.S. employer realized that its customers were unaware of how socially responsible the company had been. Like many companies today, Wal-Mart expected that its good deeds would speak for themselves. In fact, Wal-Mart's educational initiatives were drowned out by media overload, competitive messages, and growing negative news coverage. As far as many customers and the national media were concerned, Wal-Mart was good at providing bargain products but nothing more.

Once Wal-Mart recognized that it had to begin asserting itself into the increasingly important public discourse on responsibility, the company embarked on its "The Company We Keep" strategy to change consumer misperceptions. Wal-Mart became a co-partner in ABC's program *The Scholar*. The show was a six-week summer series showcasing a high school competition that awarded winners a full college scholarship totaling approximately $250,000. The arrangement with ABC gave Wal-Mart specific roles in each episode as well as advertising space during segment breaks. Wal-Mart's sponsorship of the series strategically fit with its ongoing Sam W. Walton Community Scholarship Program for students in towns where Wal-Mart resided.

By participating in *The Scholar,* Wal-Mart was able to continue its socially responsible platform and more directly articulate its education message to the public. As Betsy Reithemeyer, executive director of the Wal-Mart Foundation and vice president for corporate affairs, stated: "What we like about *The Scholar* is how it showcases individuals and their efforts to lift themselves up."[32] Wal-Mart's reputation repair now included amplifying the responsibility initiatives that needed more attention and exposure years earlier.

After understating oil reserves by top executives, as mentioned earlier, Royal Dutch Shell quickly recognized that it had to catch up with changing business practices if it was going to restore its imperiled reputation. Business perceptions on corporate governance radically shifted as Enron, WorldCom, and Tyco scandals revealed how boards of directors failed to take responsibility for overlooking wrongdoing. The Royal Dutch Shell dual-board structure began receiving harsh criticism for lack of management oversight and an outdated shared leadership model. A shift toward greater governance accountability took hold in business circles, and Royal Dutch Shell had to respond accordingly.

Since 1907, when "Royal Dutch" Petroleum and "Shell" Transport & Trading took over Standard Oil, the number-three oil giant had a two-board structure operating out of the United Kingdom and the Netherlands. The company's underreporting of oil and natural gas reserves prompted the dual board to task a steering committee with investigating any and all needed change. Its 2004 annual report read:

> Chaired by Lord Kerr, its remit was to consider how best to simplify the structures of the companies, the Boards and management of the Group; how to improve the decision making processes and the personal accountability of management; and how to enhance leadership of the Group. The steering group heard the views of a large number of institutional shareholders and shareholder groups and considered a wide range of solutions, in the end opting for the simplest, cleanest and clearest.[33]

The steering committee proposed the unification of the two existing parent companies, Royal Dutch and Shell Transport, under a single new parent company—Royal Dutch Shell plc. Royal Dutch Shell would now have a single, 15-person independent board headed by a nonexecutive chairman with a single chief executive. The dual-leadership structure was officially abandoned and the oil major fell into line with its competitors, who had single-board structures with one CEO overseeing operations. The Shell recovery process could now commence with fewer distractions.

Royal Dutch Shell did not stop there when seizing the shift. The *Fortune* 500 Company looked even deeper into the changing business environment and chose a surprising candidate for its new nonexecutive chairman. On August 4, 2005, the company announced that Jorma Ollila would be retiring from his post as CEO of Finnish telecom leader Nokia to join Royal Dutch Shell in June 2006.

This choice signaled two clear messages reflective of the times. First, the now single board chose an outsider with no allegiances to the tainted company leadership. Not only was Ollila a non-British and non-Dutch leader, but he also came from outside the petroleum industry. Second, the board selected an individual known for his moral integrity and transparent communications style. Ollila's leadership qualities fit well with today's see-through and tell-all business climate and could only help reverse Royal Dutch Shell's previous image of bureaucracy, bunker-like communications, and poor controls. Moreover, Ollila's reputation for turning around Nokia and sustainability oversight fit well with the future challenges facing the beleaguered oil major.

IBM, AT&T, Wal-Mart, and Royal Dutch Shell were each able to reinvent their organizations and strategies within shifting business and consumer expectations. By insisting on answers to the questions posed earlier in this section, leaders might be able to see these shifts as they approach rather than when it is too late.

Engage Third Parties

One way to ensure that a company remains aware of shifts in business climate and social perceptions is to receive input from independent third parties. These external parties are often unfettered by internal politics and offer valuable insights and perspectives. Third parties can also provide needed credibility and additional reputational equity that was lost during recent crises or stumbles.

In Chapter 5, leaders were urged to seek outside counsel or their "beacons of light." The focus differs in this stage of the recovery model. While outside advisers are recommended as sounding boards and sources of consolation when leaders face the bleak early postcrisis days, engaging third parties who can be more critical and confrontational during reputation restoration helps companies alter negative or indifferent perceptions and consider alternative ways to change course. Third parties are often more likely to be one step ahead of social, political, or economic changes that companies might overlook as they manage their day-to-day business.

Daily pressures often cause companies to find themselves isolated and impervious to external shifts in the business, political, and social environments. It is also common for some companies to become too confident and believe that stakeholders who are critical of the organization are misguided or misinformed. Food biotech company Monsanto found this out when it attempted to introduce genetically modified crops into Europe. Genetically modified organisms (GMOs) were successful in the United States, but many Europeans vehemently opposed genetically enhanced seeds. NGO Greenpeace actively campaigned against Monsanto's altered seeds, and even Prince Charles joined the protest. At the time, Monsanto had not effectively reached out to third parties for counsel and consensus building. If it had, the company may have been sensitive to recent mad cow disease scares in Europe that dramatically altered public opinion and reassessed its strategy.

In 2004, the Business Roundtable (BRT) took a bold step to rebuild public trust in CEOs. BRT is an esteemed association of CEOs who lead U.S. corporations that have over 10 million employees. As background, the image of the chief executive had precipitously declined due to questionable business ethics and transgressions. Whereas CEOs were once admired for building and growing companies, CEOs were now seen as wealth destroyers and greedy "fat cats." Past scandals involving CEOs such as Enron's Ken Lay, Tyco's Dennis Kozlowski, Adelphia's John Rigas, and WorldCom's Bernie Ebbers tarnished chief executive halos almost beyond restoration.

Unfortunately, these CEO scandals have not completely disappeared but, rather, have spread worldwide. Media mentions of CEO scandals increased 15 percent worldwide overall from 2005 to 2006. This is particularly true in Asia Pacific, where the rise in mentions of CEO scandals was 34 percent during the same 12-month period.[34]

The 160 BRT CEOs realized that they needed to put a stop to the diminishing confidence in executive leadership. They enlisted the support of a third-party academic institution to narrow the widening trust gap between leaders and the public. Together with the Darden Graduate School of Business Administration and in partnership with other leading American business school faculty, the Business Round-table Institute for Corporate Ethics was established to enhance the link between ethical behavior and business practice. Hank McKinnell, then chairman of BRT and chairman and CEO of Pfizer, noted in BRT's announcement of the center: "As the Chief Ethics Officers at our companies, we know setting and maintaining the highest ethical standards starts at the top."[35]

Working jointly with this one goal in mind, the BRT and Institute set forth clear guidelines for conducting research, developing an ethics-based curriculum, holding business ethics seminars, and providing hands-on training to current and new business leaders. Since its inception, the Institute has designed a Web-based ethics simulation training program; hosted senior executive ethics seminars; and announced the publication of best practices, case studies, and new benchmarking research. By engaging a respected independent third party with a distinctive point of view, hope for restoring leadership reputation could begin. The act of establishing the Institute underscored CEOs' concern about perceived leadership shortcomings and the need for more resources for better business ethics training.

Citigroup is another good example of an organization that sought out more than one third-party solution to repair its reputation. Citigroup's reputation suffered several setbacks after the dot-com bust. Citigroup's Salomon Smith Barney telecom analyst Jack Grubman became the poster boy for Wall Street conflicts of interest and shady dealings. In April 2003, the U.S. Securities and Exchange Commission (SEC) charged Salomon Smith Barney, along with fellow industry peers, a historic $1.4 billion to settle fraudulent research reports. Citigroup's fines were the largest of its peers. Citigroup also settled with the SEC on flawed structured finance work for fallen Enron and Dynegy.

Less than one year later, in April 2004, newly hired CEO Chuck Prince announced a record 10-year, $200 million commitment to financial education programs worldwide. The Citigroup initiative, which was a joint effort with the Citigroup Foundation, included a new Office of Financial Education led by a respected financial education expert, new advertising introducing the program (see Exhibit 6.1), a dedicated web site (www.financialeducation.citigroup.com), and paid time off for employees wanting to volunteer. In addition, Citigroup provided financial education to several third-party partners

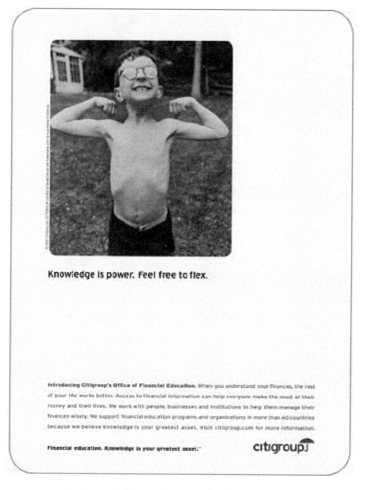

EXHIBIT **6.1** *Citibank Financial Education Campaign*

such as Junior Achievement, Operation HOPE, Rainbow/PUSH Coalition, and United Way.

A particularly helpful approach to engaging third parties is to draw analogies from other industries and consult with executives who have undergone similar problems. For example, an understanding of how oil majors managed their reputations as consumers grew angrier over rising fuel costs and industry profits could provide new insights for those in the health care business. Food company executives faced with obesity challenges could probably draw valuable lessons from tobacco industry executives.

In fact, in 2004, the Pharmaceutical Research and Manufacturers of America held a conference to discuss how to improve the industry's troubled reputation and manage the onslaught of public scrutiny and litigation. One of the guest speakers was an unlikely candidate—Altria's Senior Vice President of Corporate Affairs Steven Parrish. Altria is the parent company of Philip Morris and other consumer product and service companies.

Parrish provided sound advice from his experience overseeing Altria's resurrected image. As reported in *The Economist*, "Mr. Parrish advised drug firms to abandon their bunker mentality and engage with their critics. Rather than arguing about the past, he said, it is better to move on and give people something new to think about."[36] Parrish advised the pharmaceutical industry to be careful about doing all the talking and giving the impression that they are one large interest group. This meeting of pharmaceutical and tobacco giant executives demonstrates how the most insightful counsel can come from the most unlikely places.

Once reputations are in crisis mode, it is often too late to begin building relationships with third parties. Management guru Ram Charan describes how the best leaders synthesize information all around them: "Some leaders do this by deliberately seeking out diverse perspectives and listening to a wide variety of sources. They meet regularly with other top CEOs to bounce ideas off one another; they regularly read not just magazines and newspapers, but also Weblogs; they attend confabs like the annual World Economic Forum at Davos."[37] Listening to one's own heartbeat and not feeling the pulse of the greater business community can restrict a company's understanding of the world and limit its ability to respond quickly and effectively when necessary.

CEOs are not alone in needing outside counsel and points of view in order to restore image. In March 1968, President Lyndon Johnson's administration and the country's reputation were in shreds due to the unpopular Vietnam War. Johnson asked former top national security officials of several administrations, retired generals, and leading citizens for their thoughts on the United States' involvement in Vietnam. This informal advisory group, known as the "Wise Men," advised the beleaguered president to change course on the war's direction. That is ultimately what Johnson did when, days later, he withdrew his name for reelection and restricted further North Vietnamese bombings.[38] Outside third parties can often help leaders see beyond their immediate inner circles and receive unfiltered information.

Similarly, a final report was delivered in December 2006 to President George W. Bush on the direction of the war in Iraq. At the urging of several members of Congress, with approval from the White House, distinguished Americans gathered together to form the Iraq Study Group (ISG) under the leadership of co-chairs James A. Baker III, former secretary of state and honorary chairman of the Baker Institute, and Lee H. Hamilton, former congressman and director of the Woodrow Wilson International Center for Scholars. Other bipartisan members of the ISG included Robert M. Gates, Vernon E. Jordan Jr., Edwin Meese III, Sandra Day O'Connor, Leon E. Panetta, William J. Perry, Charles S. Robb, and Alan K. Simpson.

To decide on the best course of action, several organizations facilitated the work, nearly 50 people served in four expert working groups, four days were spent on the ground in Iraq, and 136 people were interviewed inside and outside the government.[39] As the Iraq war continued to divide the country and erode America's reputation abroad, President Bush now had the perspective of a wider group of advisers than he had before. The ISG report apprised President Bush of the increasingly grave situation in

Iraq and the urgent need to resolve the situation through greater political collaboration. The third-party report provided the president with counsel besides that given by his closest advisers.

Although the president did not adopt the study group's findings in full, he was affected by them. He selected an ISG expert to serve as one of his closest advisers. On November 8, 2006, President Bush nominated Texas A&M University President Dr. Robert M. Gates to replace Donald Rumsfeld as secretary of defense. In his November 11, 2006, radio address, President Bush stated that Gates's ISG experience would "provide a fresh outlook on our strategy in Iraq."[40]

Companies can begin mending their reputations by seeking third-party support and validation from outside company or institutional walls. Companies should also seriously consider their own board of directors, as discussed in the next section.

Recruit Your Board

To avoid corporate tunnel vision, board members need to take a greater role in defending company reputation and actively attending to matters outside the boardroom. After all, board members are now predominantly independent and can offer a wealth of outside perspective and insights. At present, boards are not being used as effectively as they could. Many board members of publicly traded companies primarily receive their information from the CEO or other senior company officers. Few board members will mention that they learned about the companies they oversee through informal stakeholder feedback or media coverage.

Management guru Peter Drucker once said that in every single business failure over the past several decades, the board was the last to know when a company was in trouble. More insights and counsel are needed from seasoned board members to guide leaders through the landmines of reputation recovery.

As described earlier, turnaround outsider CEO Ed Breen was brought in from Motorola to restore Tyco's bottom line and severely tarnished reputation. Breen immediately focused on Tyco's dysfunctional corporate governance structure. Within days of being named CEO, Breen retained Michael Useem, a director at the Wharton Center for Leadership and Change Management and corporate governance expert at the University of Pennsylvania's Wharton School.

In Breen's first letter to employees, as cited in *South Florida Business Journal,* he announced the independent professor's arrival: "Michael Useem will help Tyco develop corporate governance objectives, assess Tyco's practices as compared to the best corporate practices, make specific recommendations and work with Breen and his board to make changes."[41] The selection of Wharton's highly regarded and often-quoted Useem provided Tyco with quick and credible access to governance lessons from other companies and to ethical guidelines that could be instituted throughout the company.

Board members are often overlooked but always important allies in the war to recoup reputation losses and detect business shifts that might not otherwise be identified. Their engagement should be expanded during times of crisis.

STEP 9: BRAVE THE MEDIA

The media is no longer what it once was. At one time, companies were largely dependent on select business newspapers, magazines, and major broadcast networks to convey their message to the public. With the ubiquity of the Internet and powerful social networks, traditional media has lost some of its status as the single most powerful intermediary. Referred to as the disintermediation of the media, this revolutionary change carries both benefits and disadvantages for companies in reputation trouble.

Companies now have numerous channels to get their messages heard without exclusively relying on the major media as they did in the past. In addition to traditional media, companies now have their own web sites, text messaging, blogs, online ads, YouTube videos, and word-of-mouth marketing. As never seen before, companies are increasingly less dependent on national and local media, including the evening news, to defend themselves when they are in the spotlight.

On the downside, however, companies now have to worry about how a minor glitch can unexpectedly boil over into headline news once it surfaces online. The challenge for companies trying to restore their reputations is to know how and when to strategically use these new media outlets to their advantage and keep their reputations from spiraling further downward.

Invent New Pipelines

Beginning in 2003 and 2004, GM's falling market share, job cuts, and labor union problems dominated the media. The world's largest automotive manufacturer was frustrated by the fact that its turnaround message was increasingly overshadowed by the media's constant coverage of its financial difficulties. GM sought a new pipeline to communicate its value to customers—the general public.

At about the same time, the new world of blogging was taking hold, although most *Fortune* 500 companies continued to overlook it. GM's management decided to try something new to engage customers. In time for the 2005 January automotive show, GM launched a blog for internal and external audiences titled "fastlane.com," with Vice Chairman Bob Lutz as its first poster boy.

Fastlane described itself as "your source for the latest, greatest musings of GM leaders on topics relevant to the company, the industry and the global economy, and—most of all—to our customers and other car enthusiasts. We look forward to an open exchange of viewpoints and welcome your ideas and feedback throughout 2005."[42] On day one, Fastlane received 5,000 visitors, [43] and the number of visitors since then has increased steadily. Fastlane is paying dividends in more ways than can be imagined. It is widely read by employees and helps recruit talent to the Big Three automotive company.

Perhaps unintentionally, GM took smart advantage of the rapidly evolving communications revolution. Fastlane hosts Lutz and other executives quickly learned that the GM blog could serve as its own direct mouthpiece to the public. GM did not have to be held hostage to the mass media and could get its own side of the story out to target audiences as they pleased. In fact, the GM blog became its own news feed, with GM statements picked up verbatim by the media. By taking the risk to join the user-generated media movement circling the globe, GM discovered its own opportunity to engage directly in two-way conversations with its most valued customers. It also found its own source for strategic communications to help smooth its battered reputation.

GM and other companies in crisis are changing course in their response to the heavy downpours of criticism—some justifiable, of course. They are braving the media by starting to set the record straight on their own terms, in their own ways, and in their own words. Rumors circulated in the spring of 2006 that GM's CEO Rick Waggoner would be ousted by summer due to a slower-than-expected turnaround and investor impatience. In an unusual response to critics, GM's Vice Chairman Robert Lutz countered that the turnaround was on track: "We are removing the gloves at G.M. and are going to be much more aggressive about telling our side of the story. It's time to strike back."[44]

Lutz also fiercely defended the GM chairman and CEO: "Mark my words, read my lips: Rick Waggoner will preside over the turnaround."[45] The traditional, reactive style of corporate communications where censured CEOs and senior officers always turn the other cheek is starting to fade. Companies are beginning to adopt the political campaign model of publicly defending their reputations, using all the channels and talent at their disposal, and filling the void that used to be taken up with "no comment."

Wal-Mart also has found several new pipelines to strategically communicate its turnaround. In April 2005, the mega-retailer held a media summit in its own hometown of Bentonville, Arkansas. Over 50 journalists joined the retailer for two days. CEO Lee Scott was joined by other Wal-Mart executives to demonstrate that "we want to send a signal to you that we want to be open to you in the media, and we want to get to know you."[46] Wal-Mart decided to confront face to face one of its fiercest critics on its own territory. This is another example of a company's adapting to the changing media environment and trying to put itself on an equal footing with the media.

Companies have become very innovative in their reputation recovery outlets. During Martha Stewart's legal troubles for insider trading, the home diva began a web site called www.marthatalks.com. The web site contained several sections: "Read My Letter," "E-mail Martha," "Notes to Martha," "Other Voices," and "Setting the Record Straight." Martha discovered her own personal voice outside the Omnimedia company she founded and provided a channel for supporters' messages that could be heard by the media. Her web site was a smart, strategic way to communicate and rally stakeholders during the notorious trial. It also provided her legal team with an opportunity to set the record straight outside of the ensuing media circus. The site received over nine million hits and nearly 50,000 visitors several days after its launch.[47]

Don't Believe Your Own Propaganda—Bring in the Critics

Reality can be a difficult pill to swallow for companies accustomed to having their own way and often the final say. Facing up to the hard, cruel facts that created the initial reputation failure can be very painful, especially when it comes from the fiercest critics. Yet there is no better time to put a company's house in order than when a company is humbled and eager to get its reputation back on track. Just showing stakeholders that the company understands what went wrong and is willing to take its licks like everyone else can go a long way to restoring reputation. One way to keep the repair process moving ahead is to ignore one's own propaganda.

While it is important to bring allies and those who are sympathetic to company goals into the recovery process, it is also important to welcome those resisters who have not bought into the party line. A company's constructive critics should be brought in and not pushed away. Not every critic is going to agree with how a company changes its ways, and some may refuse to cooperate, but many will be more than willing to lend a hand with their unfettered opinion during the restoration process. Most importantly, critics keep companies from believing their own half-truths.

When new CEO Daniel Mudd took over the disgraced Fannie Mae, he had the unenviable task of restoring its dented image. Fannie Mae, a private shareholder-owned company that provides Americans with mortgage money, was scandalized by accounting improprieties under the reign of its prior CEO Franklin Raines. In his first year, Mudd met with the company's fiercest critics such as author Peter Wallison, who powerfully advocated taking away Fannie Mae's government charter, and U.S. Representative Richard Baker, who forcefully campaigned for tighter government scrutiny. Mudd's approach to restoring Fannie Mae's credibility by listening to these naysayers and embracing their opinions was called "a strategy of small gestures."[48] Mudd understood that sometimes the small head nods make a world of difference and keep companies from digging in their heels.

Similar to the small gestures of Fannie Mae's new CEO, Disney's newly appointed leader Robert Iger knew that the Walt Disney Company had lost its luster through the trials and tribulations of former CEO Michael Eisner's leadership. Disney's share price was stalling, and executive defections were piling up as Iger first took charge. Although just as immersed in Disney politics and perspective as Eisner, Iger met with the entertainment company's two most vocal critics—Apple's and Pixar's disgruntled Steve Jobs, and dissident board members Roy Disney and Stanley Gold.

Under Eisner, Disney and Pixar Animation's 14-year relationship had painfully fallen apart. The Disney-Gold rebellion against Eisner's leadership left board members feuding and the executive team distracted.[49] Iger knew that the repair process would only begin by reaching a truce with these highly influential individuals whose feuds with Eisner were widely chronicled. Iger's concessions and cease-fire with Eisner's critics were key factors in Disney's restoration of its once-storied reputation.

Critical voices do not have to come only from the outside. As Ford Motor Company began restoring and rebuilding its reputation in 2006 with its Way Forward and Bold Moves campaigns, Chairman and CEO Bill Ford asked his inner circle to critique his own leadership.[50] The automotive company could not afford another stalled turnaround, and Bill Ford wanted to make sure that everyone's cards were on the table as the team began the repair process in earnest.

He knew that listening to his own voice was not moving the failing company far enough. It was a bold move to send the message that the company was more important than his personal feelings or internal propaganda. These internal voices may have accelerated Bill Ford's decision to hire a seasoned turnaround CEO like Alan Mulally to run Ford.

Unfortunately, the business climate is often not level, fair, or consistent. Leadership has to have sufficient sense to identify shifting public opinion, ensure that its communications are in sync with changing expectations and behavior, and remain receptive to constructive criticism from traditional and untraditional sources. Risk-free communications are hard to come by when reputations are bruised, corporate vision is blurry, and company actions are placed under the microscope. The saying that necessity is the mother of invention can be applied to communications strategies when companies find that the cards are not in their favor.

CONCLUSION

The final stage of reputation recovery is now in sight. A new culture is rising, attention is being paid to outside forces and critics, and new avenues of communications are being paved to reach critical stakeholders. The next phase of reputation recovery is to make momentum known, dig in for the long-term, and stay ahead of the vortex.

CHAPTER 7

RECOVER

"We are off the crutches. But we are not running yet."

—Stuart Rose, CEO, Marks & Spencer[1]

"In short, once we got back on our feet, shook off the stigma of squandering a seemingly unassailable leadership position, and decided that just maybe our best days were yet to come, the IBM team responded magnificently—just as it had through even the darkest days early in the transformation."

Louis V. Gerstner Jr., former IBM CEO[2]

The well-known High Street institution Marks & Spencer (M&S) had seen better days. In 2004, the once-heralded UK retailer suffered from a dowdy image, executive churn, poor customer service, and fierce competition. A leading online BBC commentator was even prompted to ask, "Is Marks & Spencer's Decline Terminal?"[3]

In a dramatic boardroom shake-up later that year, M&S ousted its leadership and rehired Stuart Rose as chief executive. Rose had quit M&S in 1989 after spending 17 years to take on leadership positions at Burton Group, Argos, and Arcadia. Soon after Rose's arrival, a bitter takeover bid for M&S ensued with Arcadia's retail billionaire tycoon Philip Green. Although the new chief executive successfully fought off the hostile offer, the British newspapers embarrassingly covered the personal skirmishes in the battle for M&S in great detail. Rose ultimately successfully outmaneuvered Green's bid by boldly announcing a three-year recovery plan that included returning £2.3 billion to shareholders, closing unprofitable stores, and returning to its female-focused roots. The new CEO pledged to return M&S back to its customers!

Fast forward to January 2007, after Christmas sales were officially tallied. M&S preprofits were up nearly 33 percent, and 12,000 employees received nice boosts in their company saving plans. Share price hit an all-time high, and the company neared $2 billion in profits. M&S Chief Executive Rose declared that the famous retailer was officially in "recovery" by finally using the long anticipated "R" word (although "a small r"). Rose told the *Financial Times*: "We are out of intensive care. Now we have to get super-fit."[4]

Rose simply stated his recovery strategy: "We are doing product, environment and service."[5] While emphasizing the basics, Rose ambitiously expanded the M&S brand into electronics and other new products, super-efficient supply chains, and global markets. The chief executive also announced a radical and leading environmental program that continues to attract headlines.

Rose did not rush flashy signs of progress. He knew from past experience that recovery can never be guaranteed: "We have been in this sort of territory before. We recovered and we promptly unrecovered. We have had two [doom] cycles [under Sir Richard Greenbury and then Roger Holmes] and I want to break that. I don't want it to become a bad habit,"[6] Rose explained. He understood that to rebuild a strong brand, he needs a steady, unwavering stream of proof.

M&S is among the shining examples of the final stage of restoring reputation in this 12-step model—Recovery. After getting the company back on its feet, identifying where it stumbled, instilling a new culture, measuring progress, and communicating tirelessly, the once-failed organization can begin enjoying the fruits of its labor.

Although conditions may steadily improve, the slippery slope still appears in the rearview mirror. In some cases, companies might hear enthusiastic applause for the first time, although they should not let praise distract them from restoring their good name. As IBM CEO Sam Palmisano said about the company's recovery, "Once things got better, there was another kind of danger: that we would slip back into complacency."[7]

This chapter looks at the last three steps of recovering reputation—building momentum, recognizing the permanency of the campaign, and establishing a process for minimizing future organizational risk.

STEP 10: BUILD A DRUMBEAT OF GOOD NEWS

After months or even years of less-than-good news, many companies find themselves ready to turn the corner toward vigorously restoring their good names. Recovering reputation typically does not come from one major event or announcement, but rather from a series of small incremental steps that slowly generate positive momentum. At this stage, companies must be cautious not to appear too boastful or overconfident as good news surfaces. Companies on the recovery continuum should remain humble and always on guard.

Make It Simple

Reputation recovery should be accompanied by clear communications from the top. A rebounding company needs leadership that articulates a disciplined, straightforward, and easy-to-absorb message. M&S CEO Rose's "product, environment and service" is a good example. At this stage, recovering companies often formally centralize communications with direct reporting lines into the CEO's office. A centralized and unified communications strategy involves responding quickly, cohesively, and consistently when any emerging negative issues or criticisms arise. Companies cannot afford the risk of ad hoc or complex communications as they recover reputation.

When Royal Dutch Shell Chief Executive Jeroen van der Veer began turning around the oil giant after oil reserve discrepancies were revealed, he knew that leadership communications had to be succinct and easy to understand. "This is not the time for complicated stories."[8] The chief executive explained in an interview at The Hague that "more upstream, profitable downstream" would be the mantra for restoring the company's tarnished reputation. This message was easily understood by employees, senior team leaders, board members, customers, and shareholders. Van der Veer's call to action was simple and differentiating—increase upstream exploration and production business while profiting from downstream oil products and chemicals.

Ford Motor Company has witnessed its fair share of reputation downfalls in recent years. In 2004 and 2005, the *Fortune* 500 firm lost North American market share and reputation as measured in the America's Most Admired Companies survey. In July 2006, Toyota exceeded Ford in sales for the first time in the United States. Finally, Chairman and then-CEO William Ford unveiled his simple turnaround strategy, the "Way Forward," to restore Ford's prominence and profitability. His message was eminently clear—Ford will take more risks, choose different paths forward, and restore trust in the blue oval.

North American Ford CEO Mark Fields linked his region's turnaround plan to Bill Ford's risk-taking manifest by using a "Red, White and Bold" message. The Bold Moves campaign is consistently being used in Ford's marketing communications and achieving some staying power. The simple act of repeatedly echoing Bold Moves in advertising, web sites, and communications, along with its newly hired CEO, has built a surge of hope for the beleaguered manufacturer.

Use Symbolic Acts

Communications should not be limited to words alone. Symbolic acts serve as powerful signs that corporate recovery is in progress and change is in the air. President Reagan was the master of symbolism as he strove to repair his image in early 1987 during the Iran-Contra problems.

During his last two years in office, Reagan was regarded as a lame duck. To signal command at the end of his sagging presidency, Reagan personally presented economic news, regardless of how minor it might appear to the public or media. Moreover, the former president paid strict attention to reporters' press conference questions to show that he was not deaf to public concerns. In a smartly symbolic move, President Reagan would cup his ear when boarding Marine One to show that he was trying to hear reporters' questions that were shouted at him over the helicopter blades' deafening noise.[9]

When Tyco's Ed Breen took over from disgraced former CEO Dennis Kozlowski, it was clear that his actions would have to speak louder than the words filling newspapers every day about Tyco's errant ways. Breen's symbolic decision to move Tyco's opulent offices in New York to a less auspicious facility in West Windsor, New Jersey, helped to understatedly displace Kozlowski's lavish spending. Additionally, Breen addressed employees with confident and poised body language.[10] Certainty and tranquility are important leadership images to convey when companies are undergoing significant transformations. When CEOs look glum or worried, rumors and innuendo spread like wildfire, and employees look for the exits.

New York Stock Exchange (NYSE) interim CEO John Reed kept a low profile in the months following the ouster of previous chieftain and highly paid Dick Grasso. In a purely symbolic gesture, Reed made news by turning down the chance to light the Big Board's annual Christmas tree and ring the bell heralding each trading day's open and close. The interim CEO's actions underscored that he was more concerned with focusing on overhauling the exchange's governance structure and searching for a permanent NYSE chief executive. Reed's message was that he had a big job to do in a short time, with no time to waste.

Equally dramatic, Procter & Gamble (P&G) CEO Alan Lafley replaced the hallowed 11th floor that housed division presidents and former CEOs with a worldwide training center when handed the reins at floundering P&G several years ago.[11] Lafley's historic move to reorganize the 50-year-old building shortly after his appointment coincided with the company's first sales increase in seven years. Without having to speak a single word, the new chief signaled that P&G would be doing things differently as it turned its first corner in its comeback. These symbolic acts successfully hinted that a flatter organization was going to play a prominent role in the company's revival.

Entergy quietly used two symbolic acts to underscore how New Orleans and the company were getting back on solid ground after the devastation of Hurricane Katrina in New Orleans. According to Sandra Alstadt, director of utility communications, a strong signal of renewal was sent when Entergy crews returned to the city for the first time. These linemen became heroes in restoring faith in the city and demonstrating that Entergy was doing its job under the most difficult circumstances. The second event that reassured residents that some normalcy could be restored was the lighting of the New Orleans River Bridge.[12]

Small acts can carry a heavy weight. As new Boeing CEO James McNerney dug deep into restoring the aircraft manufacturer's reputation after several highly publicized ethical lapses, he replaced Chicago's "World Headquarters" label with "corporate offices." Although not earth-shattering, the subtle change sent a resounding message that pomposity would no longer be associated with the Boeing name.[13] Large or small, unspoken messages can signal needed change to key stakeholders watching for genuine signs of recovery.

Make Signs of Progress Visible

If recovery is on the horizon, observable signs need to be made evident. Neither profit results nor share price are always leading indicators of a turnaround. Management must find other proof points to consistently demonstrate that upward momentum exists at the tarnished company. Former Ford automotive Corporate Communications Officer Jon Harmon talks about the importance of "reputational momentum" as a means to define the art of the possible.[14] According to Harmon, this is particularly important to employees who have weathered a long drought of positive news. For stakeholders to believe and spread good word-of-mouth again, positive news must slowly begin replacing or exceeding negative news.

Another good example of making recovery visible comes from previously discussed Tyco International. When it was time to formally declare that the recovery process was officially in place, new CEO Breen initiated two noteworthy advertising campaigns. The first introduced

Tyco's brand-new 13-person leadership team that replaced the entire previous executive team (see Exhibit 7.1). The advertising targeted to Wall Street, legislators, and employees featured the following statement accompanied by individual executive's signatures: "We signed on because we believe Tyco has a bright future. We signed below to show you we mean it." The signatures underscored the point that these executives had personally signed up for the mission.

EXHIBIT **7.1** *Tyco International's Senior Team Advertisement*

Source: Tyco International and Hill Holiday.

The campaign underscored how Tyco's new leadership team was standing shoulder to shoulder behind Tyco's improving reputation. The 13-person team portrait also communicated that new leadership was focused on the team, not the individual. According to Jim Harman, Tyco International's vice president of advertising and branding, "The message behind this campaign was that Tyco had hired senior managers with the highest level of integrity from diverse manufacturing companies."[15] The advertising served as a reminder to influential stakeholders that Tyco was well on its way to rebuilding the reputation it lost.

EXHIBIT 7.2 *Tyco International's Advertising Campaign*

Source: Tyco International and Hill Holiday.

Nearly one year later, Tyco was moving forward, trimming debt, and improving its credit rating. To distance itself from its troubled past and communicate that the company had stabilized, Tyco launched its second advertising campaign using the slogan: "You may not know everything we make. But everything we make is vital."[16] The advertising listed all Tyco products, with an emphasis through its shading of one particularly critical product such as pediatric monitoring equipment (see Exhibit 7.2). Tyco was once again publicly reminding stakeholders through its advertising that Tyco was a company worth knowing better and proud to be stepping back into the spotlight.

The second corporate campaign was another first step toward cautiously but visibly shedding its past. Advertising firm Hill Holliday's CEO Mike Sheehan remarked that the communications effort was just a start. "We've helped communicate the prologue and now this is chapter one."[17] The first series of advertisements showcasing Tyco's new team was followed months later by a new corporate positioning that raised confidence in Breen's leadership and the company's momentum-building transformation.

If reputation recovery progress is being made and employees are being inspired, companies will have an easier time accelerating the momentum needed to push forward. Companies should start small but relentlessly build momentum until it catches fire and spreads exponentially.

STEP 11: COMMIT TO A MARATHON, NOT A SPRINT

IBM's recovery under former CEO Lou Gerstner was built on the understanding that reputation recovery is a long-term process that does not end after a quick burst of success. Too many companies appear to recover, only to stumble soon afterwards. For this reason, stakeholders do not regard recovery as certain until a successful track record is long in place. Even so, recovery is a continual process. Weber Shandwick's *Safeguarding Reputation* research found that crisis-ridden companies need at least seven positive quarters before declaring that a turnaround is approaching.[18]

When Sir Howard Stringer became Sony's CEO in 2005, the Wales-born company outsider knew that he was taking on a potential career buster. To give himself every chance of success, Stringer sought out the retired Gerstner for advice (as discussed in Chapter 5). Gerstner told Stringer about the long journey to recovery: "When you're transforming a company, and you're really trying to drive fundamental change, early success is both your best friend and your best enemy."[19] Early wins build confidence and silence nay-sayers, at least temporarily, but can also give the false impression that fundamental change is not needed. As Gerstner made clear, transformation should never be regarded as anything less than a marathon.

When McKesson CEO John Hammergren faced rebuilding his company's reputation, financial credibility, and employee morale, he knew that he needed to focus himself and employees on the long road ahead.

> The first, very quickly, was the realization that this was going to be a long march—not one of those quick turnaround stories. In my experience, quick turnarounds are usually financial rather than cultural and performance turnarounds. And a quick turnaround, typically involving some kind of financial engineering, doesn't necessarily position a company for success. McKesson had been around for 172 years, so my goal was to make sure it could sustain itself for another 172. I knew that the turnaround was going to take years, not months, and I needed to get that point across.[20]

Hard as it may be to accept, leaders should recognize the permanency of a recovery campaign. Recovery is continuous, with no shortcuts or days off. Every day demands winning over the hearts and minds of employees, customers, investors, and other key stakeholders. Just as presidents and other politicians must win the vote every day, companies and their leaders must prove that their company is worth support, attention, and loyalty. The ongoing recovery and restoration of a company's reputation requires extreme patience and endurance.

As former IBM CEO Gerstner said as he looked back: "After Year One: I can say without hesitation that what came next was far more difficult. If nothing else, those first 12 to 18 months at least had the benefit of adrenaline-stoked intensity—many highs, an equal number of lows, but never time to celebrate one or dwell on the other because we were literally in a situation in which every minute counted . . . after all that initial work had been completed, we'd gotten ourselves only to the starting line. The sprint was over. Our marathon was about to begin."[21] The long haul of sustainable recovery is undeniably the hardest work of all.

Marks & Spencer's CEO Stuart Rose may never have met IBM's Gerstner, but he endorses the theme of a never-ending road to recovery: "The journey is never over, which is why I have been reluctant to say recovery, because you never finish."[22] Just when companies think they have reached the safety zone, they must force themselves to think hard about where they have come from and how fragile reputation renewal can be.

Reputation recovery is an epic voyage full of courageous daily actions, small victories, and deeds that never truly slay the twin dragons of doom and gloom. Employees and those vested in a company's turnaround can never be completely satisfied. Recovery has too many epic cycles that cannot be rushed to a final close.

STEP 12: MINIMIZE REPUTATION RISK

As the recovery progress turns the final corner and the company feels healthier, reputation risk should be faithfully monitored. The once-tarnished company has to guard against any risk of further reputation damage. Minimizing reputation risk now becomes everyone's responsibility. Several companies are highlighted in this section as examples of using best practices to stay ahead of the curve and plan for the worst-case scenario.

Stay Ahead of the Curve

Barclays Bank's reputation slipped when a series of public relations gaffes came to light and kept it behind the curve. CEO Matt Barrett took over in 1999, during a period of upheaval, losses, and bloated budgets. The non-British banker began cutting costs in order to reach his target of saving $1.4 billion by 2003. Despite success in turning around Barclays and a well-received merger with leading mortgage broker Woolrich, the venerable bank made some very public missteps that set back its reputation.

Three events that caused reputational harm occurred in quick succession. In 2003, Barrett closed 171 Barclays branches. The bank closings were predominantly in rural areas and left communities with few banking options. When customers vehemently protested, Barrett had to publicly apologize and make check-cashing arrangements with local post offices for its abandoned customers. Next came word of CEO Barrett's £1.3 million compensation at the same time as the bank was announcing layoffs and closings. Barrett's third problem was an embarrassing statement made before a parliamentary committee on credit card charges: "I don't borrow on credit cards because it's too expensive." The remark did not please the nine million UK holders of Barclaycard.[23] These gaffes made world headlines and damaged the bank's fine reputation.

As a result of these issues, Barclays established a Brand and Reputation Committee in 2004 to keep itself ahead of the reputation curve. The committee's goals are to protect the Barclays brand by reviewing issues that could negatively impact its image and also guide the bank's responsibility agenda. The Brand and Reputation Committee is a subcommittee of the Barclay Group Executive Committee. At an annual business and human rights seminar, then Vice Chair and Group Executive Director Chris Lendrum remarked:

> Our Brand and Reputation Committee has the heads of all our business lines represented, plus central functions such as risk, public policy and human resources. I chair the committee and have license to intervene in any area of Barclays work which carries significant risks or opportunities for us in terms of Corporate Social Responsibility and our reputation.[24]

The committee is also charged with overseeing any related brand issues such as sponsorships, advertising, and marketing. Setting up this type of committee ensures that reputational risk is high on the executive agenda and that the slightest discrepancy will not be overlooked.

A similarly innovative best practice for minimizing reputation risk and keeping up with rapid business shifts comes from worldwide spirits company Allied Domecq. The company sells some of the world's best-known alcohol brands (Stolichnaya, Beefeater, and Kahlua) and recognizes that promoting moderate consumption and strong social responsibility are necessary elements of an alcoholic beverage company's good corporate reputation. As the social and regulatory environment evolves worldwide, alcohol companies realize that they, too, can find themselves in the same spotlight as the tobacco companies have been.

In 2001, Allied Domecq created an advertising and marketing internal code to guide its communications. Two years later, Chief Executive Philip Bowman called for the establishment of a team of outsiders to form the Marketing Review Board to pre-review all of its marketing materials in order to reduce reputational risk and maintain standards. Allied Domecq's Marketing Review Board began with three external and four internal members. In 2004, the board's composition was changed to include three additional external members to assure greater geographic representation and external points of view.

The board's original charter was to only review alcohol advertising but that has now been expanded to include all communications. Another Review Board modification was a public commitment to inspect 100 percent of campaigns prior to launch. The latter change was prompted by a U.S. complaint from the Marin Institute about a nonvetted Sauza tequila campaign titled "Lost Modesty." The Sauza billboard was alleged to encourage irresponsible consumption that would lead to nudity and loss of inhibitions.

The Allied Domencq board meets four times annually and rotates locations around the world to gain perspective on different cultures. The six external board members include lawyers, advertising executives, a health department director, and an educational reformer. In the Marketing Review Board's annual report, case studies are provided, which identify communications reviewed, issues raised, and the board's final verdict. For example, the board discussed Beefeater's sponsorship of a Spanish jet-ski championship and American NASCAR motor racing. The debate concluded with committee decisions to end the jet-ski sponsorship due to perceptions that it might be endorsing dangerous activities and an agreement not to sponsor NASCAR because of the unfavorable connection between alcohol consumption and driving.

As Bowman states in the annual report, "Of all the initiatives I have launched since becoming Chief Executive of Allied Domecq, our independent external Marketing Review Board is one of the most important."[25] Despite internal criticism that an external review board would delay advertising, suppress creativity, and give competitors an advantage, the board has been successful. A broader perspective, new insights, and healthy debate have all worked to Allied Domecq's advantage in sustaining its reputation and competitiveness in the marketplace.

Well-regarded Colgate-Palmolive Chairman and CEO Reuben Mark has a simple method for minimizing reputational risk. In his office, CEO Mark receives red transparent folders of "situation alerts" for any company problems within 24 hours of their occurrence.[26] These alerts range from an employee injury to a competitor's price change. Other top executives also get the red folders. Understandably, CEOs can be so easily distracted by the natural order of business that they overlook looming problems and early warning signs. Stories abound about companies ignoring repeated pleas to attend to potential disasters or listen to someone who could have forestalled trouble. At Colgate-Palmolive, these red folders help to keep those risks to a minimum.

A new wave of officers has emerged as companies combat reputational risk and achieve financial stability. When Fannie Mae was charged with violating accounting rules in 2004, the Office of Federal Housing Enterprise Oversight named a chief risk officer to monitor future operations.[27] Years ago, chief risk officers (CROs) worked primarily for large banking institutions. Today, CROs are in great demand across all industries as business grows more complex and regulatory pressures rise.[28] A 2005 Economist Intelligence Unit (EIU) survey found that 24 percent of all global firms intend to hire a CRO in the next two years.[29]

CROs are not only growing in number but also in influence as they begin playing a broader role than previously seen. In addition to managing capital risk, reporting risk to the board, and ensuring regulatory compliance, CROs are being asked to serve as ombudsmen within their organizations. In addition to evaluating accounting practices and staying informed of regulatory requirements, they closely monitor reports of unethical conduct, discriminatory practices, and employee mistreatment. The EIU survey also found that monitoring and identifying emerging risks will increase in importance in their job responsibilities over the next three years.[30]

Former Toyota President Fujio Cho told *BusinessWeek* in 1999 that "We will not be caught off guard."[31] To prevent problems from cropping up and harming the automotive company's reputation, Toyota's 250,000 employees share values and problems through the Toyota Way, its prized method to manage quality and execute with perfection.

Toyota's management principles described in the Toyota Way are based on getting quality right the first time. If employees see a problem on the assembly line, they must stop production and fix the problem the same day. Part of Toyota's way to minimize risk to its high-quality reputation is to ask "why" five times about every problem. The brainchild of Toyota founder Kiichiro Toyoda's father in the 1930s and made popular in the 1970s by the Toyota Production System (TPS), this simple, five-why rule is deeply embedded in the Toyota mind-set.

Toyota TPS pioneer Taiichi Ohno remarked that "Having no problems is the biggest problem of all."[32] Problems are regarded as opportunities in disguise. Ohno instructed staff to personally explore problems and persist until their root cause is revealed. He used the example of a welding robot to encourage asking "why" five times:

1. Why did the robot stop? The circuit has overloaded, causing a fuse to blow.
2. Why is the circuit overloaded? There was insufficient lubrication on the bearings, so they locked up.
3. Why was there insufficient lubrication on the bearings? The oil pump on the robot is not circulating sufficient oil.

4. Why is the pump not circulating sufficient oil? The pump intake is clogged with metal shavings.

5. Why is the intake clogged with metal shavings? Because there is no filter on the pump.[33]

Asking why five times is not a superficial cliché. Toyota workers lessen the chances of something becoming a long-term problem by doing their "why-whys." As experience has shown Toyota, it usually takes five inquiries until no new information appears and the problem is solved.

Interestingly, Toyota has recently experienced quality problems. The car manufacturer has had to recall over nine million cars in the United States and Japan since 2004, a 27 percent increase. In the summer of 2006, president Katsuaki Watanabe bowed deeply to apologize for the quality lapse. Additionally, Watanabe gave more power to its Customer First Committee. This group analyzes problems regardless of whether the problem is customer service, parts, design, or manufacturing.[34] Toyota is insistent on reducing its reputational risk now before the problems continue much longer and truly harm its reputational leadership.

Staying ahead of the curve also requires borrowing strategies from other industries and institutions. Hospitals provide companies with good examples of preparing for trouble. Many emergency rooms once issued "code blue" alerts when a patient underwent cardiac arrest.[35] The code blue signal alerted the resuscitation team to attend to the ailing individual. Hospitals soon came to realize that cardiac symptoms were frequently present before patients' hearts began to fail and that nurses were often in better positions than others to detect these hard-to-detect danger signs. Some of these earlier symptoms that nurses mentioned after patient heart attacks tended to be more qualitative than quantitative.

To maximize patients' survival rates and reduce the number of code blues, hospitals surveyed nurses and then gave them lists of early heart attack signs that are often overlooked. Hospitals also gave nurses the authority to call special rapid-response teams into action when they believed symptoms appeared. Although some of these rapid-response alerts did not require intervention, medical staffs were now aware of what to anticipate and how to prepare for heart problems in the future.

Plan for the Worst-Case Scenario

As described earlier, minimizing risk by always keeping your eyes firmly on the horizon can be managed in many ways. This includes planning for the worst-case scenario that could set the company back several steps or nearly back to the beginning when the crisis first struck.

Royal Dutch Shell has been in the business of scenario planning for more than three decades (www.shell.com/scenarios). Its highly regarded Global Scenarios are developed by the Shell Scenario team, along with contributions from external experts from around the world. The impressive list of outside individuals contributing to the series demonstrates Shell's willingness to draw insights wherever they originate.

In the spirit of collaboration, Shell freely shares its scenarios and, in fact, they can be purchased on Amazon.com. As described by Shell CEO Jeroen van der Veer: "These scenarios are different from forecasts in that they provide a tool that helps us to explore the many complex business environments in which we work and the factors that drive changes and developments in those environments."[36]

As described in the 2025 scenarios report, the events of 9/11 and the breakdown of trust from corporate scandals profoundly influenced markets, states, and society forever. Shell applied these scenario learnings to its own situation in repairing perceptions of its transparency, disclosure guidelines, and governance structures. As Shell repairs its tarnished reputation of the past few years, its scenario planning helps the company make sense of the world and gives it a sharp competitive advantage.

Another organization that engages in scenario planning to prevent myopia is the National Intelligence Council (NIC).[37] In an attempt to better understand the role of the United States globally and prepare for the unpredictable, the NIC produces community-wide forecasts of issues and challenges facing U.S. security. As noted on its web site, "In an attempt to engage creative thinking from outside the intelligence community's classified bunker, the NIC has increasingly participated in joint sponsorship of conferences with non-governmental institutions and has produced a number of unclassified publications. . . . "[38]

The NIC consults many experts from around the world and gathers regionally to compose a true global view of the next 15 years. The NIC's 2020 project involved more than 1,000 nongovernmental experts, and they created four possible world scenarios that might profoundly affect business, society, and politics. Again, this information is freely available for those companies hoping to stay just one step ahead of approaching disasters.

One corporate communications officer of a large European insurance company uses a straightforward method that has worked for the company over many years. Every week he submits to the CEO a list of the problems that have arisen over the past seven days. These issues can range from small to large. The officer assigns a number from 1 to 10 to each problem, indicating its chances of becoming extremely dangerous to not too dangerous to the company's business and reputation. Each problem shown to the CEO contains a brief strategy to minimize damage if it were to mushroom into a critical situation.

Every quarter, the corporate communications officer reviews the inventoried risk portfolio and identifies the worst-case scenario that has the potential to severely damage the company. The communications department readies a detailed and complete strategy with preventative measures that could diminish the crisis if it actually happened. Both the CEO and the chief corporate communications officer find their weekly and quarterly risk portfolio plan helpful to predicting any danger underfoot.

Pharmaceutical giant GlaxoSmithKline found itself under the harsh media spotlight when its leading antidepressant Paxil was linked to teen suicide. Its CEO Jean-Pierre Garnier realized that building new drug pipelines comes with major risks. To ensure that he sees any potential crisis before it turns menacing, Garnier now always seeks an outside perspective.

When asked in *Fortune* how he deals with continual unfolding crises such as the Paxil problem, he revealed a common-sense strategy: "I've hired someone from outside the industry, whom I call an angel. I said to myself, 'Maybe I'm too close to this. I want you from the outside to tell me things we do that could potentially lead to similar crises.' "[39] Garnier was not shy in asking for outside help to identify the worst-case scenario that could destroy his company's reputation. This person can come from outside the industry or be a consultant familiar with regulatory or legal matters.

Google can also help companies visualize and plan for disaster. For example, Google is building a complimentary early-warning system that scours web sites, e-mails, and other local and regional data to notify critical authorities of potential natural disasters such as bird flu, famine, earthquakes, droughts, wildfires, and floods. In contrast, early-warning signs can arise from routine observations such as what happened to Hasbro in 2006. An employee of the toy manufacturer came across a reference to the death of a two toddlers choking on a plastic toy bench screw during a customary check on Amazon.com.[40] Hasbro voluntarily recalled nearly 250,000 Team Talkin' Tool Benches after notifying the U.S. Consumer Product Safety Commission.

Minimizing risk is critical to maximizing reputation recovery. Anticipating problems should be practiced every day to avoid unforeseen problems and keep companies on the straight and narrow path to full recovery.

CONCLUSION

This chapter ends the reputation recovery journey outlined in this book. Although there are more than 12 steps for companies as they continue to rebuild and protect their reputation for the long-term, the major factors in restoring reputation have been described in detail. This author's final thoughts on the reputation landscape follow in the final chapter.

PART III

CHAPTER 8

RETURN TO FLIGHT

"Knowing first aid is not the same as protecting your health."

—Robert G. Eccles, Scott C. Newquist, and Roland Schatz,
Harvard Business Review[1]

"But every disaster has its own rhythm, which needs to be established and analysed."

—World Economic Forum 2007[2]

"They say the first 20 days are the emergency, and 10 times that, the next 200 days, are the relief, and then 10 times that, the next 2,000 days, are the recovery."

—Cholene Espinoza, former United Airlines pilot and
New Orleans fund raiser[3]

There are few absolutes in business, but when it comes to reputation, three facts are indisputable: No reputation is bulletproof, no company can afford to be reputation-blind, and no suit of armor is impenetrable enough to withstand the reputational slings and arrows directed at companies and leaders today. Higher standards of corporate governance, citizen journalism, a cynical public, and emerging pressure groups have all combined to create a new business environment in which corporate reputation has never been a more valuable and differentiating asset—or more at risk.

This book has identified the 12 steps companies can follow to preserve and recover reputation. It has addressed the multitude of reputation challenges that companies and organizations now face. There remain, however, other observations that do not easily fit within a step-by-step analysis and are worth emphasizing one more time.

After a nearly three-year waiting period following the *Columbia* space shuttle tragedy that killed all seven astronauts, NASA's shuttle *Discovery* lifted into orbit from Cape Canaveral on July 26, 2005. *Discovery* was NASA's first "return to flight" mission and was declared a success. This concluding chapter summarizes what additional perspectives are necessary to return to flight for those companies ready to soar again.

REPUTATION LOSS IS ALL BUT INEVITABLE

Reputation loss is not a one-time event that afflicts some ill-starred company that finds itself under a dark but passing cloud. It is not a sudden emergency to be dealt with and then forgotten. Reputation failure has become a part of doingz business each and every day.

Reputation failure is no longer a threat that looms large only for companies in high-risk industries and activities. It has become an all-too-familiar scenario for highly admired companies in all corners of the world. In 2006, one-third of the Global *Fortune 500*—the world's largest companies—experienced deterioration in their "most admired" status from the previous year.[4] Moreover, Weber Shandwick's *Safeguarding Reputation*™ research found that approximately one out of three global business leaders believe it is likely that their company will sustain reputation damage within the next two years.[5]

If one thing is certain, it is that losing reputation is more common than ever before and is here to stay. As noted in Chapter 2, nearly 9 out of 10 global business executives agreed that there has been a growing trend of corporate reputation damage.[6] In 2006, there were 270 mentions of "reputation risk" in the global media compared with only two mentions in 1990—135 times more (see Exhibit 8.1).

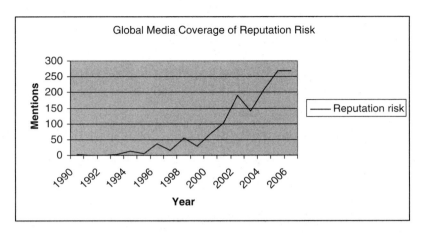

EXHIBIT **8.1**   *Global Media Coverage of "Reputation Risk"*

Source: Weber Shandwick Factiva proprietary analysis, 2007.

An astonishing 32 million mentions of "risk" conferences surfaced on Google[7] in April 2007, and chief risk officers are now cited as one of the most sought-after positions in business. The threat of reputation damage lurks around every bend in the road to business success. Companies must never underestimate their vulnerability or the severe cost of even the slightest misstep.

With such gusty headwinds sweeping across the business landscape, this book was written as a practical guide for companies striving to maintain their reputational equilibrium. Although following the 12 steps will increase a company's ability to avoid reputation loss or at least reduce its adverse effects, it is no guarantee that reputation loss will not occur. It is nearly impossible for companies to foresee the many surprising twists and turns that lay ahead as they seek reputation sanctuaries. Reputation loss increasingly appears all but inevitable.

Who could have foreseen most-admired BP attracting headlines for deathly explosions and not for reduced carbon-dioxide emissions? Who could have imagined that the oil company that educated the world about global warming and also educated millions about global carbon footprints would lose its green halo? How could giant Sony, the product innovator and savvy marketer extraordinaire, have lost reputation capital over lithium-ion battery packs costing less than

$100? Let's not overlook sassy start-up carrier JetBlue either. It would have been inconceivable to many JetBlue fans that *BusinessWeek* would knock the airline off its inaugural 2007 Customer Service Champs listing because of delays and cancellations when a severe winter storm chilled its service reputation.[8]

REPUTATION RECOVERY COMES WITH NO EXPIRATION DATE

Reputation recovery is an ongoing process. Although research indicates that it takes about four years for a company to recover its lost reputation, there is no guarantee that trouble, large or small, is not lurking around the corner. Restoring a company's good name is a continuous journey.

Entergy's subsidiary in New Orleans faced painful reputation repercussions as restoration costs soared and its customer base dramatically diminished. Once customers realized that there would be rate increases, the honeymoon soured. Entergy also became a political punching bag for populist candidates running for political office. The company is now just beginning to feel that it has turned a corner. Federal aid arrived, Entergy New Orleans emerged out of bankruptcy in early June 2007, and a compromise phasing in of rate increases was approved. As Sandra Alstadt, Entergy's director of utility communications, looks back on the past two years of rebuilding in New Orleans, she notes that the recovery process is ongoing and never ending.[9] Without fail, another hurricane season comes around every 12 months.

When CEO Ed Zander arrived at Motorola, the company's reputation was at an all-time low, with quality problems, financial issues, and missed launch dates. More than one year later, with the raging success of the sleek Razr cell phone, Motorola blew the lid off expectations. Three years later, Zander found himself facing three straight missed quarters and a downturn in the mobile phone business.

As Zander experienced firsthand, reputation recovery is rarely a straight path to success. In these hyperfast and challenging times, reputations rise and fall all the time. Companies and their leaders have to come to grips with the idea that reputation building is inexhaustible. It may take four years[10] to recover from major problems but there are no guarantees that it will not require continued massive intervention to keep the momentum going to achieve lasting results.

REPUTATION WOUNDS ARE OFTEN SELF-INFLICTED

Many of the causes of reputation loss appear self-inflicted. As identified in Weber Shandwick's *Safeguarding Reputation*™ research, the top three triggers leading to reputation injury—financial irregularities, unethical behavior, and executive misconduct—are all issues that could have been prevented if companies only had better controls in place.

Every day, offline and online sources broadcast the latest news and updates on the ethical failings and errors in judgment of senior business leaders. Unfortunately, they do not lack for examples. As of December 2005, the Corporate Fraud Task Force obtained more than 1,000 corporate fraud convictions, and convicted 92 corporate presidents, 82 chief executive officers, 40 chief financial officers, 14 chief operating officers, 98 vice presidents, and 17 corporate counsel or attorneys.[11] Neither are transgressions limited to the United States. In Japan, a country that serves as a model for crime control, shock waves went through the business community when Internet portal Livedoor was accused of inflating results.

As boards take on greater oversight of executive activity and decision making and governments continue to punish offenders, the number of internal executive misdeeds should gradually diminish. Better corporate governance rules and independence should now provide the requisite checks and balances that were missing several years ago. Furthermore, an increase in companies led by separate chairmen or lead directors serves as an additional watchdog on internal irregularities and executive excess. With greater regulations in place, and luck, self-inflicted reputation wounds might wind down in the years to come.

NEW REPUTATION PERILS LIE AHEAD

Besides widespread executive wrongdoing, some triggers of reputation failure are especially strong candidates for escalation in the years ahead. Several of these surfaced in *Safeguarding Reputation*™ and deserve to be watched:

- *Security breaches.* The growing sophistication of online pirates, absence of foolproof protection methods for confidential online data, and pervasive power of the Internet have all converged to create an environment ripe for reputational risk. According to www.attrition.org/dataloss, which tracks lost and stolen data around the world, there have been more than 136 million global data breaches since 2000. Notably, this surge in security breaches prompted Fujitsu, the world's third largest information technology (IT) services provider, to highlight the seriousness of this threat in an advertising campaign focusing on IT system security.

- *Environmental violations.* Consumer and environmental rights groups are increasingly sensitive and alert to environmental violations such as rainforest deforestation, oil spills, pesticide consumption, human rights abuses, and pollution. The penalties for these violations can be severe—in terms of both monetary fines and reputation loss.

  In the future, we may see an increase in criminal charges levied against senior officers and employees for various environmental transgressions. As a preventative measure, companies should implement rigorous training and audits of their environmental operations.

- *Product recalls.* Health and safety issues continue to plague consumer and food product companies. From E. coli and Salmonella contamination to defective technology components, recalls and their resulting negative reputation backlash are on the rise. In Europe, the number of reported recalls of dangerous and faulty consumer goods more than doubled in 2005, according to European Commission (EC) figures analyzed by PricewaterhouseCoopers.[12] By the end of December 2005, an average of two recalls per day were being posted on the EC web site, with 706 reports filed (an overall 126 percent increase in reported recalls since figures were first compiled in 2004).

In the United States, the 2006 spinach crisis (E. coli contamination) was a dramatic example of the dire consequences that a product recall can have on brand reputation. The outbreak, which most tragically caused three deaths and 104 hospitalizations, resulted in losses of nearly $200 million. The company identified as the source of the outbreak saw a 70 percent drop in sales of its nonorganic bagged salads, with the local spinach industry likely to lose a third of its $180 million revenue.[13] As this book was being finalized, product recalls of tainted toys, toothpaste and pet food that were made in China monopolized headlines and caused considerable damage to the emerging country's reputation.

- *Regulatory noncompliance.* Companies around the globe are now required to adhere to new compliance legislation—the Sarbanes-Oxley Act in the United States, the New EU Transparency Directive for all EU member states, and J-SOX in Japan. This new business climate is making organizations of all types and sizes far more vulnerable to reputation risk.

  When reports of a company's noncompliance find their way to customers, investors, and other stakeholders, as well as to the media and the general public, they have far-reaching consequences for both corporate reputation and the bottom line. In the future, reputations will be built on public expectations as much as compliance with laws and regulations.

New reputation threats are always on the horizon. The possibility of a pandemic outbreak could have severe consequences for the reputations of ill-prepared companies. To prepare for such a frightening epidemic, Lehman Brothers has been testing its ability to keep its business operating by installing hot lines for traders to communicate with one another, regardless of circumstances.[14]

In 2006, 70 British firms simulated a multimonth flu epidemic to assess how well the financial services sector could manage by relying on employees working at home. The Financial Services Authority head of Business Continuity Management concluded, "It's easier said than done."[15] If such a worldwide horrific event should occur, company reputations might transform overnight, as the world saw with Hurricane Katrina, severe acute respiratory syndrome (SARS), and September 11.

REPUTATION RADAR IS NOT A LUXURY

Investing in reputation radar to identify and track potential company threats or problems is no longer a "nice to have" but a necessity for twenty-first-century companies. In the years ahead, companies will install increasingly sophisticated reputation radar and dashboards that alert them to emerging issues across products, regions, competitors, and industries.

U.S. toy companies who imported manufactured products made in China might have foreseen trouble ahead when Chinese-made pet food was found to be tainted with poisonous chemicals. Moreover, food companies might have predicted the onslaught of criticism directed at them from the rising media focus on obesity. Armed with systems to identify emerging warning signs, companies can begin managing their overall communications messages to decrease negative public opinion.

Business news and information services provider Factiva offers several tools to help companies understand what is being said about them in the traditional media and on influential web sites, discussion boards, and blogs. Factiva's fact-based tools help companies spot emerging issues, shifts, and trends that migrate and mutate through consumer-generated and mainstream media.[16] Factiva also provides an hourly media service for executives charged with managing breaking news and crises. These reputation dashboards can be designed to detect issues or problems that will soon need attention.

At Factiva Insight, a product for media measurement uses new discovery technology that has the ability to identify company-identified terms that might sharply increase in media conversations, blogs, discussions groups, and other channels. This tool alerts companies to spikes in conversations that contain emerging problems and that have otherwise remained dormant until erupting. A team of analysts reviews all the phrases where specific terms surface and determines whether companies should be alerted and perhaps take action.

According to Dow Jones's Enterprise Media Group Global Practice Director Chris Shaw, this discovery technology identified the Apple iPod screen scratch issue early on. The media team analyzed a cluster of conversations around the iPod and was able to flag the scratched screen problem. Shaw said, "Discovery technology can help a company assess what might look like an innocuous comment but actually needs immediate attention."[17] This type of reputation radar is a tool that can keep a company ahead of the crisis or at least prepared.

With the burgeoning Internet and blogosphere, companies will soon have many more options available to them to manage reputation. New reputation management companies are surfacing daily. Visible Technologies is an example of a new search engine reputation management company that helps companies manage "outdated or erroneous information" to ensure "that fair and accurate information is correctly ranked among the top 20 results on each site when people search for your company, products and services, or executive management team."[18] Companies or individuals work with Visible Technologies to replace misdeeds with good deeds. Another new reputation company is ReputationDefender, whose stated goal is to "watch your back."[19] The company defends the reputations of professionals, job seekers, employers, college applicants, and children. ReputationDefender searches and destroys negative content about individuals by asking myspace.com or blogs to erase specific information and tracking down people who post negative mentions.

REPUTATION HALOS DO NOT MAKE YOU A SAINT

Admired reputations can blind some companies to risk. JetBlue's customer friendliness and low fares helped the airline grow quickly. The carrier received rave reviews for its individual seat-back televisions, amenities, and quality customer service. Founder and then-CEO David Neeleman was even spotted in an attendant's apron, serving passengers. However, when a winter ice storm hit the U.S. Northeast in February 2007, hundreds of JetBlue passengers found themselves stranded and delayed for days. The media rightfully ravaged JetBlue for the lack of a workable crisis contingency plan. When asked how this debacle could have happened, CEO Neeleman replied, "Lack of a contingency plan. When you run as good as we have run, I don't think you're as good at [crisis management.]"[20]

Clearly, JetBlue's stellar reputation erroneously led the company to believe it was invincible. Despite Neeleman's near-textbook-perfect handling of the crisis by, among other efforts, humbly apologizing for the 1,000+ flight cancellations, JetBlue must still win back lost passengers and earn new accolades. Luckily for JetBlue, the airline's previous fine reputation offers some residual benefits from substantial goodwill and near fanatical customers. Even so, damage has been done and JetBlue must focus anew on its reputation building.

JetBlue's experience is a warning to even the most highly regarded companies. A blue-ribbon reputation today may give companies additional time to stave off a crisis, but it does not make a company immune. International Institute for Management Development (IMD) Professor Phil Rosenzweig has written about the extreme dangers of the halo effect. He describes how lasting success is an illusion and that "there's a strong tendency for extreme performance in one time period to be followed by less extreme performance in the next."[21] Since there are so few long-term successful companies, companies should be on the alert that their angelic reputations do not mask inner demons.

REPUTATION IS AND ALWAYS WILL BE A JOB FOR CEOs

"Managing image and company reputation is one of the more obvious jobs of the CEO," said former GE CEO Jack Welch.[22] Despite a gradual increase in chief reputation officers like myself, the job of managing reputation ultimately belongs to the CEO. In the years ahead, reputation will only be more complex and all-encompassing to manage. Reputation "war rooms" similar to Wal-Mart's, where experts manage the company's image campaign, will be a standard feature at corporate headquarters. The most successful CEOs will not only be those who can choose wisely between black and white but also between different shades of gray.

We should expect that future CEO-elects will be selected based in part on effective communications skills to maneuver around increasingly treacherous reputation waters. It is not inconceivable that future CEOs will come from the ranks of chief public relations and corporate communications officers. Few CEOs with communications backgrounds now come to mind other than David D'Alessandro, former chairman and CEO of John Hancock Financial Services and former president of Manulife Financial Corporation. It is also not inconceivable that boards will increasingly look for members who have deep public relations experience and can counsel CEOs dealing with crises and critics. The professionally trained public relations CEO, president, or prime minister might not be too far off.

Wal-Mart's CEO, Lee Scott, is a good example of a CEO whose communications skills have been sorely tested by the constant pummeling of the giant retailer's reputation. Despite his background as a humble, low-key leader like founder Sam Walton, Scott has had to be more assertive in recent years. His role as a more outward reputation defender and guardian was forced on him when Wal-Mart faced increasing criticism over employee wages, hiring practices, and health care benefits. *Wall Street Journal* columnist Alan Murray noted Scott's transformation:

> No one exemplifies the new CEO more than Wal-Mart Chief Executive Lee Scott. When Mr. Scott found his company under attack by a well-organized political campaign, he responded in kind. He reached out to his opponents, took polls of opinion leaders and hired political consultants. He also embraced environmentally friendly policies, improved employee healthcare coverage and began advocating policies like an increase in the minimum wage.[23]

A critical factor in Wal-Mart's success depends on how well Scott, with input from the board and senior management, steers the company through its precarious waters ahead. In the not-too-distant future, boards may limit their CEO successor searches to those with time-tested wounds from fresh reputation battles.

Another example comes from Citigroup's CEO Chuck Prince. He soon realized that the job Sandy Weill handed him in 2003 required more from him than maintaining the status quo and his legal expertise. A focus on leadership integrity and communications transparency was needed. A behind-the-scenes counselor and modest by training, Prince soon learned that his humble ways were not bold enough for leading Citigroup through a series of reputational challenges that found the company making headlines.

Post-Enron, many CEOs like Prince shunned the spotlight to avoid the celebrity CEO label. When times get tough, however, CEOs are required to make the calls that restore trust and confidence in the companies they lead. As Citigroup's troubles escalated, Prince commented: "I'm not used to operating in the limelight but the difficulty of the moment demanded it. I had to get out front and say, 'we're going in this direction, follow me.' "[24]

On the heels of the Japanese regulatory problems described earlier in Chapter 4, Prince made the eye-popping decision to adopt a new leadership style that extended his presence beyond the corner suite. Speaking about his discomfort with a more public profile both internally and externally, Prince said, "I have to be able to inspire people, to motivate people. That's my job. It cuts against traditional patterns of doing business, it's new, and it feels awkward at first."[25] As emphasized several times in this book, CEOs must be the first line of protection when reputations are damaged and devote considerable energy and effort to defending their company's good names.

BEYOND THE BOTTOM LINE

Corporate responsibility has not always played an influential role in reputation management and recovery. For example, famed Nobel Laureate and economist Milton Friedman once asked whether corporate executives have responsibilities in their business activities other than to make as much money for their stockholders as possible. His answer was a resounding no. Times have clearly changed. People now regard a broader corporate responsibility as fundamental to the society in which they live. It also serves as a strong industry-differentiating feature for prospective employees and a powerful source of motivation for current employees.

Many leaders now recognize that the international business community, as well as the world at large, judge companies on more than financial performance, and that corporate responsibility has risen to a new level of importance. Companies have awakened to the fact that corporate responsibility is a business imperative in building and preserving a good reputation.

Corporate responsibility's favorable impact on reputation will continue to make it a legitimate and permanent feature of the business landscape. Research by Professors Karen Schneitz of Pepperdine University and Marc Epstein of Rice University found that socially responsible companies are protected during crises from greater financial losses.[26] Moreover, the vast majority of global business executives (79 percent) in Weber Shandwick's research reported that companies with strong corporate responsibility track records recovered their reputations faster postcrisis than those with weaker records.[27]

As social, economic, and political agendas increasingly influence consumer and market issues, companies will only continue to recognize that a record of corporate responsibility is more than a bandage to be applied when injury appears. It can inoculate a company against long-term reputation failure. To benefit society, it must be a wholesale change in the way companies manage their business. Responsibility is no longer an accessory to reputation building. It is now and will only increasingly become a must-have corporate mandate.

REPUTATION CAPITAL RULES

As intangible assets such as reputation grow in importance and are viewed as a company's most valued and competitive asset, the practice of reputation sustainability and recovery will grow in stature. An explosion in reputation experts has only just begun. There were more mentions in 2006 of reputation experts or specialists in the global media than in the entire decade of the 1990s. Nearly every day, there is a new reputation inquiry made to this author by a hedge fund, actuary, journalist, management consultant, or insurance risk executive. In 2006, this author received more telephone calls about companies interested in hiring corporate reputation managers and directors than in any year before.

Years ago, reputation expert Charles Fombrun and I would chuckle about our small circle of reputation experts that barely comprised a handful. With the Internet and increasing reputational challenges facing companies, a whole new wave of reputation experts, companies, and seers are arriving.

Everyone—including companies and their leaders—deserves a second chance. The same goes for companies and leaders who have lost reputation. Just as people learn from the past, offending companies should be given the chance to rehabilitate themselves for the sake of employees, customers, investors, and other important stakeholders. If a company has built up equity in its trust bank, the opportunity to redress mistakes should be granted. The truth is that second chances can be the opportunities of a lifetime.

This final chapter of *Corporate Reputation* has reflected on the future of reputation. As the saying goes, second chances are rarely a matter of luck. Getting a second chance takes blood, sweat, and tears. If companies follow this book's steps to recovery, they should be able to navigate the difficult terrain of reputation loss and never leave their reputations up to the roll of the dice.

NOTES

PREFACE

1. Charles Fombrun, *Reputation: Realizing Value from the Corporate Image* (Cambridge, MA: Harvard Business School Press, 1996).
2. Jim Collins, "High Returns Amid Low Expectations," *Wall Street Journal*, February 11, 2002.
3. Leslie Gaines-Ross, *CEO Capital: A Guide to Building CEO Reputation and Company Success* (New York: John Wiley & Sons, 2004).
4. Nathaniel Hawthorne, *The Scarlet Letter* (New York: Modern Library Classics, 2000): 29.

CHAPTER 1

1. Chairman Alan Greenspan, Commencement Address, Harvard University, Cambridge, MA, June 10, 1999.
2. Peter J. Firestein, "Building and Protecting Corporate Reputation," *Strategy & Leadership* 34, no. 4 (2006): 25.
3. Stacey Plaisance, "New Orleans, Tourism Officials Tout Mardi Gras' Economic Success," Associated Press Newswires, February 26, 2007.
4. Editorial, "In Divided New Orleans," *New York Times*, May 15, 2007.
5. Available from: www.cbsnews.com/stories/2005/09/08/opinion/polls/printable824591.shtml.
6. Id.
7. Id.
8. Weber Shandwick, *Safeguarding Reputation*™ with KRC Research, 2006.

161

9. Roger C. Vergin and M. W. Qoronfleh, "Corporate Reputation and the Stock Market," *Business Horizons 41*, no. 1 (1998): 19–26.

10. Daniel Simon, "Happy Employees, Happy Customers: Understanding the Relationship between Work-Life Policies, Labor Market Opportunities, and Customer Satisfaction," Cornell University Department of Applied Economics & Management, 2002.

11. Joanne Cleaver, "Lust for Lists," *Workforce*, May 2003: 44–48.

12. Id.

13. Weber Shandwick proprietary analysis, 2007.

CHAPTER 2

1. Brier Dudley, "Microsoft at Midlife: Microsoft CEO Wants Company to Broaden Its Reach, Burnish Its Reputation," *Seattle Times*, February 24, 2003.

2. Available from: www.walmart.com.

3. Most Admired Companies Survey, *Fortune*, March 3, 2003.

4. "New National Zogby Poll Finds Americans Hold Diverse, Strong, & Increasingly Negative Opinions about Wal-Mart," Press Release, December 1, 2005. Available from: www.zogby.com.

5. Lauren Etter, "Gauging the Wal-Mart Effect," *Wall Street Journal*, December 3–4, 2005.

6. "The Intangible Revolution," Institute of Practitioners in Advertising, 2006.

7. Id.

8. Chris Woodcock, "Why Reputation Is a Major Factor in Business Continuity Management." Available from: www.continuitycentral.com/feature 0335.htm.

9. Weber Shandwick, *Safeguarding Reputation*™ with KRC Research, 2006.

10. "Reputation: Risk of Risks," An Economist Intelligence Unit Executive Summary, 2005.

11. *See* note 9.

12. David J. Rothkopf, "When the Buzz Bites Back," *Washington Post*, May 11, 2003.

13. Id.

14. Available from: www2.coca-cola.com/contactus/myths_rumors/index.html.

15. Chip Cummins, "Shell Wages Legal Fight over Web Domain Name," *Wall Street Journal*, June 2, 2005.

16. Available from: http://slate.msn.com/id/2102723/.

17. Merissa Marr, "For Michael Moore, Controversy Is Marketing," *Wall Street Journal*, May 18, 2007.
18. David Blum, "Black Days at Black Rock," *New York*, February 7, 2005: 31.
19. John Passacantando, Executive Director, Greenpeace USA, Arthur W. Page Annual Spring Meeting, April 12, 2007.
20. *See* note 10.
21. Available from: www.citigroup.com/citigroup/features/data/weill 021008.pdf.
22. Available from: www.awpagesociety.com.
23. Weber Shandwick, *New Wave of Advocacy*™ with KRC Research, 2007.
24. Deborah Mattinson and Graeme Trayner, "Connecting with Voters: How Business Can Learn from New Thinking in Political Research," Opinion Leader Research, presented at the Annual Conference of the Market Research Society, March 11–12, 2004.
25. Id.
26. Alison Maitland, "Business Bows to Growing Pressures," *Financial Times*, November 29, 2004.

CHAPTER 3

1. Phil Watts, Royal Dutch Shell, "Earning Trust—Creating Value from Brand and Reputation," 10th Annual Marketers' City Lecture, London, September 25, 2002.
2. Maria Bartiromo, "Neeleman Explains Himself," *Business Week*, March 5, 2007.
3. Available from: www.xerox.com/Static_HTML/annualreport/009. htm.
4. Id.
5. Weber Shandwick, *Safeguarding Reputation*™ with KRC Research, 2006.
6. Id.
7. Louis V. Gerstner Jr., *Who Says Elephants Can't Dance?* (New York: HarperBusiness, 2002).
8. GE 2002 Annual Report, Letter to Shareholders.
9. Leslie Gaines-Ross, *CEO Capital: A Guide to Building CEO Reputation and Company Success* (New York: John Wiley & Sons, 2003).
10. Rory F. Knight and Deborah J. Pretty, "Reputation & Value: The Case of Corporate Catastrophes," Oxford Metrica. Available from: www.oxfordmetrica.com.

11. *See* note 5.
12. "Reputation: Risk of Risks," An Economist Intelligence Unit Executive Summary, 2005.
13. Jack Welch with John A. Byrne, *Jack: Straight from the Gut* (New York: Warner Books, 2001): 385.
14. Weber Shandwick, *CEO Departures.*™ Available from: www .webershandwick.com.
15. Joann S. Lublin and Erin White, "More Outside Directors Taking Lead in Crisis," *Wall Street Journal*, March 19, 2007.
16. Id.
17. Press Release, March 13, 2005. Available from: www.disney.go .com.

CHAPTER 4

1. Carlos Ghosn and Philippe Ries, *Shift: Inside Nissan's Historic Revival* (New York: Currency, 2005): 210.
2. Nelson D. Schwartz, "Can BP Bounce Back?" *Fortune*, October 16, 2006: 93.
3. Mike Hughlett, "New Chief Reconnecting Motorola," *Chicago Tribune*, January 2, 2005.
4. Sue Herrera, "BP—CEO Interview," CNBC/Dow Jones Business Video, March 24, 2005.
5. "Texas Tragedy Leaves Cracks in BP's Image," *International Petroleum Finance* 8, June 2005.
6. Anne Belli, "Safety Board Failure of BP Alarms," *Houston Chronicle*, June 29, 2005.
7. Update on Chemical Safety Board's Investigation, *Houston Chronicle*, June 28, 2005. Available from: www.chron.com/cs/CDA/ssistory.mpl/special/05/blast/3182510.
8. BP Products North America to Open New Office in Texas City, July 1, 2005. Available from: http://bpresponse.org/external/index.cfm?cid=946&fuseaction=EXTERNAL.docview&documentID=78034.
9. Nelson D. Schwartz, "Can BP Bounce Back?" *Fortune*, October 16, 2006: 92.
10. Jad Mouawad, "BP Replacing Head of Alaska Operations," *New York Times*, November 2, 2006.
11. Steven Mufson, "BP Failed on Safety, Report Says," washington post.com, January 17, 2007.
12. Anne Belli, "BP Flaws Unattended for Years," *Houston Chronicle*, January 17, 2007.

13. John M. Biers, "After Texas Blast, BP Works to Heal Ties with Social Funds," Dow Jones Newswires, May 25, 2005.
14. *See* note 9.
15. Leslie Gaines-Ross, *CEO Capital: A Guide to Building CEO Reputation and Company Success* (New York: John Wiley & Sons, 2003).
16. "An Open Letter to McDonald's Customers," *Chicago Tribune*, August 22, 2001.
17. Id.
18. "Work or Be Fired," *Globe and Mail*, August 4, 1981.
19. "U.S. Air Controllers Warned of Reprisals If They Strike Today," *Globe and Mail*, August 3, 1981.
20. *See* note 18.
21. Associated Press–NBC News Telephone Poll, *New York Times* Abstracts, August 16, 1981.
22. Larissa Tiedens, Fiona Lee, and Christopher Peterson, "Admitting Missteps May Boost Stock Prices," August 2004. Available from: www.gsb.stanford.edu/news/research/ob_corpresponsibility .shtml.
23. Patrick McGeehan, "Chief of Goldman Sachs Apologizes for Remarks on Firm's Productivity, "*New York Times*, February 4, 2003.
24. Lisa Yoon, "A Lesson in Public Speaking," CFO.com, February 5, 2003.
25. Personal conversation with Carol Ballock, May 15, 2005.
26. Associated Press, "Sony Apologizes for Global Battery Recall," *Mercury News*, October 24, 2006.
27. Yukari Iwatnai Kane and Phred Dvorak, "Howard Stringer, Japanese CEO," *Wall Street Journal*, March 3–4, 2007.
28. Barbara Kellerman, "When Should a Leader Apologize and When Not?" *Harvard Business Review*, April 2006: 78–79.
29. Id., p. 77.
30. William J. Holstein, "In G.M.'s Sight Lines: Washington and Tokyo," *New York Times*, December 18, 2005.
31. Available from: www.gsb.stanford.edu/news/headlines/vftt_mulcahy.shtml.
32. BPCC Teleconference, Director of Utility Communications, Sandra Alstadt, December 14, 2006.
33. Sophie Arie, "More Arrests as Parmalat Fraud Scandal Deepens," *The Guardian*, January 1, 2004.
34. Available from: www.gti.org/pressroom/articles/pr_012004.asp.
35. Id.

36. Beth Herkovits, "Connor Keeps the Red Cross One Step Ahead of Crisis," *PRWeek*, March 21, 2005.
37. David E. Sanger and David Johnston, "U.S. Officials Says Spanish Government 'Mishandled' Reports on Bombing," *New York Times*, March 18, 2004.
38. "Spain Aznar Government Slammed in Final Bombings Report," Dow Jones International News, June 22, 2005.
39. Carol Hymowitz, "There's Room for Recovery after a Bad-News Bungle," *Wall Street Journal*, January 21, 2004.
40. Id.
41. First Annual Business Ethics Conference sponsored by *Business Ethics* magazine, New York, April 20, 2005.
42. John D. Durrett, "Recovering from Crisis: An Interview with the CEO of McKesson," *McKinsey Quarterly*, 2006, no. 2.
43. "Crisis Helped to Reshape Xerox in Positive Ways," *Leadership and Change*, November 17, 2005. Available from: www.knowledge.wharton.upenn.edu.
44. Telephone conversation with Sandra Alstadt, Director of Utility Communications, Entergy, March 26, 2007.
45. Ian Bickerton, "It Is All About the Value Chain," *Financial Times*, February 24, 2006.
46. "Tyco's Edward Breen: When Leadership Means Firing Top Management and the Entire Board," *Knowledge at Wharton*, November 2005.
47. Telephone conversation with Micho Spring, February 8, 2007.
48. Arthur W. Page Society, "Page One" Conference Call, December 9, 2004.
49. Telephone conversation with Professor Jim Bright, Indiana University School of Journalism, March 23, 2007.
50. Kris Hudson, "Behind the Scenes, PR Firm Remakes Wal-Mart's Image," *Wall Street Journal,* December 7, 2006.
51. Available from: www.cbsnews.com/stories/2006/09/13/eveningnews/main2007062.shtml.
52. David Koenig, "TXU Missteps Encouraged Critics, Enraged Lawmakers," chron.com, March 25, 2007.
53. Thomas L. Friedman, "Marching with a Mouse," *New York Times*, March 16, 2007.
54. Aaron Ricadela, "Oracle vs. SAP: Sound or Fury," *BusinessWeek*, April 9, 2007.
55. Weber Shandwick, *Safeguarding Reputation*[TM] with KRC Research, 2006.

56. Ghosn and Ries, pp. 93–98.
57. Id., p. 99.
58. Id.
59. Id., p. 121.
60. Id., p. 123.
61. Nicholas George, "Ericsson Back from the Brink: Corporate Turnaround," *Financial Times*, March 29, 2005.
62. Id.
63. Louis V. Gerstner Jr., *Who Says Elephants Can't Dance?* (New York: HarperBusiness, 2002): 24.
64. Id.
65. Kurt Andersen, "St. Judy's Got to Go," *New York*, October 31, 2005.

CHAPTER 5

1. Carlos Ghosn and Philippe Ries, *Shift: Inside Nissan's Historic Revival* (New York: Currency, 2005): 117.
2. Admiral Harold Gehman, Columbia Accident Investigation Board Press Briefing, August 26, 2003, National Transportation Safety Board, Washington, DC.
3. Columbia Accident Investigation Board, Volume 1, Appendix A, August 2003 (Limited First Printing, Washington DC: National Aeronautics and Space Administration and the Government Printing Office): 231.
4. Id., p. 232.
5. Id., p. 233.
6. Columbia Accident Investigation Board, Volume 1, Chapter 7, August 2003, p. 177.
7. Columbia Accident Investigation Board, Volume 1, Chapter 6, August 2003, p. 170.
8. Admiral Harold Gehman, "Leading in an Era of Uncertainty and Change," Wharton School of Business Leadership Conference, Philadelphia, PA, June 2, 2004.
9. *See* note 2.
10. *"Dealing with Crisis: Five Leaders Speak Out,"* knowledge@wharton, www.knowledge.wharton.upenn.edu, November 17, 2005.
11. Id.
12. Henry Leutwyler, "One Tough Assignment," *Fast Company*, September 2006.
13. Marjorie Kelly, "Tyco's Ethical Makeover," *Business Ethics*, Spring 2005.

14. Nelson D. Schwartz, "Can BP Bounce Back?" *Fortune*, October 16, 2006.

15. John D. Durrett, "Recovering from Crisis: An Interview with the CEO of McKesson," *McKinsey Quarterly*, no. 2, 2006.

16. Karen W. Arenson, "What Organizations Don't Want to Know Can Hurt," *New York Times*, August 22, 2006.

17. Amy Edmonson and Mark D. Cannon, "The Hard Work of Failure Analysis," *Harvard Working Knowledge*, August 22, 2005.

18. Available from: www.nytco.com/pdf/committeereport.pdf, p. 5.

19. Available from: http://www.nytco.com/pdf/committeereport.pdf.

20. Id.

21. Id., pp. 4–5.

22. Available from: http://nytco.com/pdf/siegal-report050205.pdf.

23. Id., p. 3.

24. Byron Calame, "Preventing a Second Jayson Blair," *New York Times*, June 15, 2006.

25. Anne Belli, "BP Memo Bore Grim Prediction Weeks before Blast," *Houston Chronicle*, March 23, 2006.

26. Ann Davis, "Closing Bell: How Tide Turned Against Purcell in Struggle at Morgan Stanley," *Wall Street Journal*, June 14, 2005.

27. Jesse Eisinger, "Lear Case Shows Sometimes Investors Can Detect Crises before Management," *Wall Street Journal*, March 15, 2006.

28. Louis V. Gerstner Jr., *Who Says Elephants Can't Dance?* (New York: HarperCollins, 2002): 64.

29. David Rynecki, "Putting the Muscle Back in the Bull," *Fortune*, April 5, 2004.

30. Christopher Rhoads, "Motorola's Modernizer: CEO Zander Shakes Up VPs, Pushes Cool Phones and Vows to Leave Rivals in the Dust," *Wall Street Journal*, June 23, 2000.

31. Available from: www.evolve24.com/4_news.html.

32. Available from: http://loosewire.typepad.com/blog/2003/12/electronic_voti.html.

33. Weber Shandwick, *Safeguarding Reputation*™ with KRC Research, 2006.

34. E-mail communication with Jonathan Carson, CEO, Nielsen Buzz-metrics, March 23, 2007.

35. Id.

36. "Computer Associates: Clearing a Cloud: How John Swainson Is Remaking the Scandal-Plagued Company," available from: http://knowledge.wharton.upenn.edu, November 2005.

37. Yukari Iwatani Kane and Phred Dvorak, "Howard Stringer, Japanese CEO," *Wall Street Journal*, March 3–4, 2007.
38. E-mail communication with Joy Sever, June 8, 2007.
39. Id.
40. Philip J. Kitchen and Andrew Laurence, "Corporate Reputation: An Eight-Country Analysis," *Corporate Reputation Review* 6 (2003): 103–117.
41. Gerstner, 2002, p. 223.
42. Peter Kim, The Forrester Wave™: Brand Monitoring Q3, September 13, 2006, Available from: www.nielsenbuzzmetrics.com/downloads/whitepapers/Forrester_BrandMonitoringWaveReport.pdf.
43. Available from: www.technorati.com/about/.

CHAPTER 6

1. Monica Langley, "Inside Mulally's 'War Room': A Radical Overhaul of Ford," *Wall Street Journal*, December 22, 2006.
2. Fiona Colquhoun, Nonexecutive director at DIEU, www.dieu.com.
3. Available from: http://money.cnn.com/magazines/fortune/globalmostadmired/2007/industries/industry_1.html.
4. Stanley Holmes, "Cleaning Up Boeing," *BusinessWeek*, March 13, 2006.
5. Id.
6. Available from: www.boeing.com.
7. Peter Robison and James Gunsalus, "Boeing Chief Tackles Ethics, All-New Jet," *Seattle Post-Intelligencer*, May 29, 2006.
8. Rhonda L. Rundle, "Tenet CEO Tries to Erase Effects of Scandals," *Wall Street Journal*, July 8, 2006.
9. Louis V. Gerstner Jr., *Who Says Elephants Can't Dance?* (New York: HarperCollins, 2002): 182
10. Chip Cummins and Almar Latour, "Changing Drill: How Shell's Move to Revamp Culture Ended in Scandal," *Wall Street Journal*, November 2, 2004.
11. Id.
12. Rod Arnott, "Royal Dutch Shell: Putting at Risk Reputation as a Resource." Available from: www.oxfordenergy.org/pdfs/ShellAuditComment.pdf.
13. "When Something Is Rotten," *The Economist*, July 25, 2002.
14. John D. Durrett, "Recovering from Crisis: An Interview with the CEO of McKesson," *McKinsey Quarterly*, 2006, no. 2.
15. *See* note 13.

16. Chip Cummins and Guy Chazan, "Risk Taking Shell CEO Stays in the Race," *Wall Street Journal*, March 29, 2007.
17. Available from: www.godrej.com/gstory/change/2006/janfeb/Work Practices.htm.
18. William M. Bulkeley, "Back from the Brink," *Wall Street Journal*, April 24, 2006.
19. Available from: www.ignet.gov/pande/faec/gallupsurveybackground.pdf.
20. Rodd Wagner and James K. Harter, *12: The Elements of Great Managing* (Washington, DC: The Gallup Organization, 2006).
21. "Gallup Publishes Long-Awaited Follow-Up to Bestselling Management Book," press release, www.gallup.com, November 8, 2006.
22. Allison Overholt, "New Leaders, New Agenda," *Fast Company*, May 2002.
23. William C. Symonds, "Staples: Riding High on Small Biz," *BusinessWeek* Online Extra, April 5, 2004.
24. Paul Hemp and Thomas A. Stewart, "Leading Change When Business Is Good," *Harvard Business Review*, December 2004.
25. Gerstner, 2002, p. 117.
26. Id., p. 119.
27. Telephone conversation with Laura Schoen, February 5, 2007.
28. Dick Martin, "Your Good Name before You Lose It," *Across the Board*, November/December 2004.
29. Dick Martin, *Tough Calls: AT&T and the Hard Lessons Learned from the Telecom Wars* (New York: AMACOM, 2005).
30. "AT&T: Whose Company Is It?" PBS Online Newshour Transcript, April 29, 1996.
31. *See* note 28.
32. Stuart Elliott, "Wal-Mart's New Realm: Reality TV," *New York Times*, June 3, 2005.
33. Royal Dutch Petroleum Company Annual Report and Accounts 2004, Unification of Royal Dutch and Shell Transport, www.shell.com/html/investor-en/reports2004/rd/struc_gov/unification_rd_st.htm.
34. Weber Shandwick proprietary analysis, June 14, 2007.
35. "Business Roundtable Unveils First-of-Its-Kind Initiative on Ethics," Business Roundtable, www.businessroundtable.org, January 14, 2004.
36. "Got a Match?" *The Economist*, November 27, 2004.
37. Ram Charan, "Sharpening Your Business Acumen," *strategy+business*, Spring 2006, no. 42.

38. George Packer, "Not Wise," *The New Yorker*, May 8, 2006.
39. Available from: www.usip.org/isg/about.html.
40. Available from: http://usgovinfo.about.com/od/defenseandsecurity/a/isg.htm.
41. "Tyco CEO Addresses Employees," *South Florida Business Journal*, August 2, 2002.
42. Available from: www.fastlane.gmblogs.com.
43. Available from: http://bcom522.blogspot.com/2007/04/blogging-done-right-general-motors.html.
44. Jeremy W. Peters, "G.M. Vice Chairman Rebuffs Critics of Turn-around," *New York Times*, April 13, 2006.
45. Id.
46. John N. Frank, "Wal-Mart Goes after Critics at First-Ever Media Summit," *PR Week*, April 11, 2005.
47. Editor, "Martha Talks in the Dog House," www.brandchannel.com, May 11, 2006.
48. Annys Shin, "Fannie Mae's Repairman: CEO Daniel H. Mudd Must Fix Problems with Accounting and Culture," *Washington Post*, November 16, 2005.
49. Laura M. Holson, "Disney Renovation," *New York Times*, August 15, 2005.
50. Micheline Maynard, "Job 1: Make His Day," *New York Times*, April 30, 2006.

CHAPTER 7

1. Elizabeth Rigby, "Retail's Ruthless Charmer," *Financial Times*, January 13/14, 2007.
2. Louis V. Gerstner Jr., *Who Says Elephants Can't Dance?* (New York: HarperBusiness, 2002), p. 109.
3. Available from: http://news.bbc.co.uk/1/hi/business/3624961.stm.
4. *See* note 1.
5. Elizabeth Rigby, "Rose Helps M&S Live Another Day," www.ft.com, November 7, 2006.
6. *See* note 1.
7. Paul Hemp and Thomas A. Stewart, "Leading Change When Business Is Good," *Harvard Business Review*, December 2004.
8. Chip Cummins and Michael Williams, "Shell's Chief Keeps It Simple," *Wall Street Journal*, January 17, 2006.
9. Kenneth M. Duberstein, "Reagan's Second-Half Comeback," *New York Times*, November 2, 2005.

10. Joann S. Lublin and Mark Maremont, "Taking Tyco by the Tail; After a Tumultuous First Year, Breen Discusses His Strategy to Clean House, Restore Trust," *Wall Street Journal*, August 6, 2003.

11. Beth Belton, "Procter & Gamble's Renovator-in-Chief," *BusinessWeek*, December 11, 2002.

12. Telephone conversation with Sandra Alstadt, March 16, 2007.

13. Peter Robison and James Gunsalus, "Boeing Chief Tackles Ethics," *Seattle-Post Intelligencer*, May 29, 2006.

14. Telephone conversation with Jon Harmon, March 30, 2007.

15. Telephone conversation with Jim Harman, May 18, 2007.

16. Suzanne Vranica, "Tyco Aims to Put Its Woes Behind It," *Wall Street Journal*, June 15, 2004.

17. Sean Callahan, "Tyco Revitalizes Brand," *BtoB*, November 8, 2004.

18. Weber Shandwick, *Safeguarding Reputation*™ with KRC Research, 2006.

19. Richard Siklos and Martin Fackler, "Sony's Road Warrior," *New York Times*, May 28, 2006.

20. John D. Durrett, "Recovering from Crisis: An Interview with the CEO of McKesson," *McKinsey Quarterly,* 2006, no. 2.

21. *See* note 2, p. 107.

22. Tim Teeman, "He's Made M&S Bloom," *The Times*, January 11, 2007.

23. Oxford English Language Teaching, available from: www.oup.com/elt/catalogue/teachersites/oald7/newsreader/articles/credit_cards?cc=global.

24. Chris Lendrum, "Important Levers For Protecting and Upholding Human Rights Internationally?" The 2004 Business and Human Rights Seminar, London, December 9, 2004.

25. Philip Bowman, "The Chief Executive's View," Marketing Review Board Annual Report 2004/2005.

26. Paul Kaihla, "Best-Kept Secrets of the World's Best Companies," *Business 2.0*, March 16, 2006.

27. Suzanne McGee, "A Hot New Job—Chief Risk Officers," *Wall Street Journal*, www.careerjournal.com, May 9, 2005.

28. Id.

29. "Chief Risk Officers to Grown in Number and Influence," press release, Economist Intelligence Unit Survey, May 12, 2005.

30. Id.

31. Emily Thornton, "A New Order at Nissan," *BusinessWeek*, October 11, 1999.

32. Available from: www.toyota.co.jp/en/vision/traditions/mar_apr_06.html.

33. Id.

34. Michiyo Nakamoto and John Reed, "Steady Hands on a Supercharged Toyota," *Financial Times*, January 29, 2007.

35. Michael A. Roberto, Richard M. J. Bohmer, and Amy C. Edmondson, "Facing Ambiguous Threats," *Harvard Business Review*, November 2006: 112.

36. Jeroen van der Veer, "Introduction to Shell Global Scenarios to 2025," www.shell.com.

37. Geoffrey Colvin, "An Executive Risk Handbook," *Fortune*, October 3, 2005.

38. Available from: http://www.fas.org/irp/nic/index.html.

39. Abraham Lustgarten, "Wisdom from Big Pharma's Dr. Gloom," *Fortune*, March 21, 2005.

40. Annys Shin, "2 Deaths Prompt Toy Recall," washingtonpost.com, September 23, 2006.

CHAPTER 8

1. Robert G. Eccles, Scott C. Newquist, and Roland Schatz, "Reputation and its Risks," *Harvard Business Review*, February 2007.

2. Available from: www.weforum.org/en/knowledge/Events/2007/Annual Meeting/KN_SESS_SUMM_1.

3. Lisa Belkin, "From a Dark Past, a Spirit Renewed," *New York Times*, August 13, 2006.

4. Weber Shandwick proprietary analysis, 2007.

5. Weber Shandwick, *Safeguarding Reputation*™ with KRC Research, 2006.

6. Id.

7. Google search for "reputation risk," March 31, 2007.

8. "Customer Service Champs," *BusinessWeek*, March 5, 2007.

9. Telephone conversation with Sandra Alstadt, March 16, 2007.

10. *See* note 5.

11. United States Senate Committee on the Judiciary, Hedge Funds and Independent Analysts: How Independent Are Their Relationships? Testimony of Matthew Friedrich, Principal Deputy Assistant Attorney General, June 28, 2006.

12. "Consumer Product Recalls on the Rise Across Europe," press release, PriceWaterhouseCoopers, April 4, 2005.

13. Michael Y. Park, "*E. coli* Outbreak Hurts Spinach Farming Industry, Restaurants," *Fox News*, September 22, 2006.

14. "The Drawbacks of Homework," *The Economist*, December 2, 2006.

15. Id.

16. Available from: www.factiva.com.

17. Telephone conversation with Chris Shaw, April 27, 2007.

18. Available from: www.visibletechnologies.com.

19. Available from: www.reputationdefender.com.

20. Maria Bartiromo, "Neeleman Explains Himself," *BusinessWeek*, March 5, 2007.

21. Phil Rosenzweig, "The Halo Effect, and Other Managerial Delusions," *McKinsey Quarterly* 2007, no. 1.

22. Jack Welch with John A. Byrne, *Jack: Straight from the Gut* (New York: Warner Books, 2001): 394.

23. Alan Murray, "Executive's Fatal Flaw: Failing to Understand New Demands on CEOs," *Wall Street Journal*, January 4, 2007.

24. Mara Der Hovanesian, "Rewiring Chuck Prince," *BusinessWeek*, February 20, 2006.

25. Id.

26. Available from: http://fmcenter.aicpa.org/Resources/Management +Accounting+Guidelines/Executive+Summary+%E2%80%94+ Integrating+Social+and+Political+Risk+into+Management+ Decision+ Making.htm.

27. *See* note 5.

INDEX